HISTORICAL CHRISTIANITY
AFRICAN CENTERED

By James C. Anyike

Proving the vital role of black people in
establishing the Christian religion and
dispelling the myth that Christianity
is "the white man's religion."

**Also by James C. Anyike
Published by Popular Truth, Inc.:**

African American Holidays
and
Anyike's Rites of Passage Guidelines

HISTORICAL CHRISTIANITY AFRICAN CENTERED

By James C. Anyike

Popular Truth, Inc.
Chicago, Illinois

Popular Truth, Inc.
1448 East 52nd Street Box 274
Chicago, IL 60615
(312) 548-6000

Library of Congress Catalog Number 94-067222

ISBN: 0-9631547-2-9

Cover Design by Troy Brown

Edited by Derrick K. Baker

Printed by
Winston-Derek Publishers Group, Inc.
United States of America

DEDICATION

To my son

ROBERT OLUFEMI ANYIKE

May you and your generation
never cease to learn,
never cease to grow,
never cease to honor the Creator,
never cease to honor the ancestors,
never cease to honor your African heritage,
never cease to love yourself
and
never cease to change the world!

PREFACE
by Minister Greg Stanton

To my brothers and sisters on the continent of Africa and those in the diaspora, greetings in the precious name of our Lord and Savior. This preface serves as words of encouragement to the reader of this book. In the following pages you will find a primer written for all who wish to start the journey away from certain beliefs which are not substantiated by truth.

As I read the manuscript for this book repeatedly, I heard a still small voice inside saying "Truth crushed to the ground will always raise its head." Today, not only is the head rising, but the entire body is being raised by a people, who like the truth, have been crushed down by the ugliness of the Western world's Eurocentricity.

You may be pondering the relevance or need for an African centered historical approach to Christianity. You may even assume that history is always presented as "true history." However, the historians subjectivity may produce a less than accurate report of historical facts. Like many seekers of truth, I have discovered that history is often just that, "his-story." It is time that we begin to ask ourselves a few pertinent questions, such as: How is it that humanity which was formed in the "likeness" of God, from the rich soil of Southeastern Africa (Alkebulan), lost its color and resemblance to the Creator? What do the ancient biblical and hieroglyphic writings say about the indigenous dwellers of Kemit (Egypt) and the God (singular) they served? By what authority did Europeans depict biblical people as white, when they were obviously people of color? When we begin to apply the principle of Kujichagulia (self determination), we begin to break free from the heavy and burdensome chains of "his-story." We can then answer these and other important questions by utilizing the richness of African history and culture.

We live in a society where belief and truth aren't synonymous to each other. Traditionally, we are taught that Jesus was of European descent, that the Greeks were the progenitors of philosophy and high culture, and that Africans were to be "hewers of wood and drawers of water." Must I continue on? It is evident that people of African descent, and mankind as a whole have been adversely affected by racism, institutionalized Eurocentrism and a conspiracy to destroy truth. If this book is read in the spirit in which it was written, it can be the catalyst that will motivate God fearing Christians to have a richer re-birth (born again) experience in the natural. Like Paul, "I would not that you remain ignorant brothers and sisters in regards to natural things." Studying the natural and physical provides insight into the spiritual realm.

I encourage you to read this book along with a note pad and pencil. I am confident that as you read, questions will begin to develop in your mind. You will also find answers to many questions you've had, but were afraid to ask out of fear that you would be considered a heretic. If you write your questions down, you will be on the path to finding truth. The scriptures inform us that God is a rewarder of those who diligently seek him. Truth, a characteristic of God, is found only by searching and seeking. Multitudes have read the scriptures time and time again, not realizing that what they see transcends what is so evident, the truth. Only the seeker finds truth.

Because they see not; and hearing they hear not, neither, do they understand. And in them is fulfilled the prophecy of Esaias, which saith, By hearing ye shall hear, and shall not understand; and seeing ye shall see and not perceive." (Matthew 13:13-14)

I pray that as you read this book, the eyes and ears of your understanding will open, and that your voice will resound with truth. The path you now walk will be traveled with a sense of pride and sure footedness. You will realize that many of your present beliefs are anchored by blind faith (faith and faith alone). Like the man who was blind from birth, you too will say "All I know is I once was blind but now I see."

Finally brothers and sisters, I challenge you to continue the re-birthing process. When you begin to read the scriptures from the cultural context in which they were written, that which has been hidden or elusive will appear, it is TRUTH.

Standing firmly in the faith,
Minister Greg Stanton, Pastor
Exodus Ministries of Bellwood, IL

TABLE OF CONTENTS

Part IV.
RACISM AND CHRISTIAN FACTIONALISM

ACKNOWLEDGEMENTS

All praises, honor and glory to the Creator for using me to write this great book during the most difficult time of my life, and to his son, the Word of God, who is lord over my life.

Praises to my African and Native American ancestors, through whom the Creator gave me life and their spirits are a blessing to me.

The highest honor to my father and mother, Major and Bettie Brame, for first giving me life and for continuing to save my life each day through the good Christian up-bringing I received; to my grandmothers, Louise "Mudees" Brame and Mary Robertson, for being strong Christian matriarchs; to my brothers and sisters, Mary, Kwame (Donald), Maurice, Philip, Carolyn, Dorothy and Kenny, for your continued love and support; and to Lisa Anyike for your undeserved love, support and friendship.

Asante sana to Rev. Walter A. McCray, Dr. James W. Peebles, Dr. Kwame John R. Porter, Minister Greg Stanton, Omar Kenneth Johnson, Robert Vaughter, Karl Fletcher, Rev. Harry W. Cooper, Jr., Rev. Melvin Jones, Dr. Jacob Carruthers, Dr. Charles Finch III, Darrell "Imani", Carolyn Griffin, Ron Harris, Dr. Colleen Birchett, Mark Allen, Rev. Willie B. Jemison, Derrick K. Baker, Troy Brown, E.J. Bassette, Eddie Bassette, Warrine Pace, Corbin Baker, Norman Christie, Erline Arikpo, Desiree Jordan, Eddie and Clarice Read, Morgan Carter, Tyra Herrell, Coco Collins, Alfred "Coach" Powell, Loretha Cole, Billy "Ameen" Armento and Gloria Prince for the technical, financial, spiritual and moral support that you all gave to me so that I could give to others.

Lastly, a very special asante sana to Rev. Al Sampson for allowing the Creator to use you to encourage and guide me to the resources I needed to print this book, and for your continued help and advice over the years.

FOREWORD
by Dr. Kwame John R. Porter, Ph.D

This book, *Historical Christianity African Centered*, is James Anyike's second major book. His first book, *African American Holidays*, was one of the first major books, in this century, of this genre by a Black American author. Anyike joins the growing pantheon of Africans and African-Americans who are rewriting and correcting both distortions and omissions of Black people from the history of America and the world. Anyike's book on African American holidays fills in hundreds of missing facts, events and contributions by African-Americans.

In *Historical Christianity African Centered*, he joins an honored cadre of scholars who have sought to be historically truthful and factual concerning the African presence in the biblical world. Among these scholars who Anyike now joins are:
W.E.B. DuBois, Dr. Edward Blyden, Dr. Martin Delaney, James Whitfield, Bishop McNeil Turner, Dr. James W. Peebles, Dr. Charles B. Copher, Dr. Robert Bennett, Dr. Larry Murphy, Dr. Henry Mitchell, Dr. Olin P. Moyd, Dr. James H. Cone, Bishop Alfred Dunston, Dr. Joseph Johnson, Dr. Carter G. Woodson, Dr. Benjamin E. Mays, Dr. William Banks, Dr. William H. Bentley, Rev. Walter A. McCray, Dr. Cain Hope Felder, Dr. Ulysses "Duke" Jenkins, Rev. Donald Guest, Bishop Edsel A. Ammons, Dr. Nya Kwiawon Taryor Sr., J.A. Rogers, Walter Rodney, Dr. Chancellor Williams, Dr. Yvonne Delk, Dr. Jeremiah A. Wright, Dr. Hycel B. Taylor, Dr. Melvin Banks, Dr. Allan Boesak, Dr. Chiekh Anta Diop, Aylward Sorter, Dr. Tom

Skinner, Dr. Ronald Potter, Dr. Henry J. Young, Dr. Gayraud S. Wilmore, Basil Moore, Dr. Joanne Grant and others.

In this book James Anyike seeks to build on and extend the research of contemporary biblical scholars, such as Dr. Cain Hope Felder, Rev. Walter A. McCray, Dr. Charles B. Copher and Dr. James Peebles. Dr. Copher has been one of the "fathers" of African or black biblical studies since the 1950's. Rev. McCray, author and publisher (Black Light Fellowship in Chicago, IL) of *The Black Presence in the Bible*, is a disciple of Dr. Copher. Perhaps, the two most comprehensive black biblical scholars of the 1990's are Dr. James W. Peebles, publisher of the new and exciting *Original African Heritage Study Bible*, and Dr. Cain Hope Felder, senior researcher and editor for this new Bible, and author of *Troubling Biblical Waters* and *Stony the Road We Trod*. The two latter books are, perhaps, the best biblical commentaries in existence.

I should add the name of an important elder who made it possible for scholars, such as Cone, Felder and others to find collegiality and resources during their graduate study days. I speak of Dr. C. Shelby Rooks, former director of the Protestant Fellowship Fund and former president of the Chicago Theological Seminary. He is also the author of a book which chronicles a 35 year struggle in opening up graduate theological studies for African-Americans in American seminaries. Dr. Rooks did an excellent job educating predominantly white seminaries and recruiting qualified blacks for graduate theological studies. His book, *Revolution in Zion*, is also must reading. When I was the founding dean of The Chicago Center for Black Religious Studies (1971-74), Dr. Rooks and a cadre of Black religious scholars were a solace of support and inspiration.

Because Christianity, particularly its holistic and accurately validated heritage, includes Africans from its inception, my reference to these pioneers and spiritual warriors of the faith must be included in any serious dialogue on biblical studies. Anyike is a brilliant young leader under 32 years of age at this writing. His future value as a carrier and repository of this sacred trust and tradition must be nurtured and influenced by those of us now considered "scholarly elders." He is also an officer and colleague in our church, The Christ United Methodist Pan-African Pentecostal Fellowship of Chicago, IL.

Since literally thousands of books and millions of words have been written about Christianity, mostly from a Western or European frame of reference, it is very important (as I have told brother Anyike) that what we write be well documented, factual and almost irrefutable in the face of our critics, enemies and others who may charge us with using historical particularism as revisionist methods in slanting Christianity and the biblical tradition and history to exclude whites or Europeans from its history. It has been very difficult for our religious and cultural opponents to attack, with integrity, the *Original African Heritage Study Bible*. They encounter the same difficulty in attempting to discredit the well researched works of Dr. Felder, Dr. Copher, Rev. McCray, Dr. Rooks, Dr. Cone, Dr. Wilmore and others. I must also add one of the most brilliant young black philosophical/theological scholars in the world, that is Dr. Cornel West of Princeton University. West, the author of some nine books, including *Prophecy Deliverance*, *Prophetic Fragments* and *Keeping Faith*, he carries one of the sharpest intellectual and spiritual "swords" of the mind on this planet.

I have also referred brother Anyike to several African theologians and historians. Two of them, Dr. Allan Boesak, author of *Farwell to Innocence*, which describes historically and theologically the spiritual bankruptcy of white historical Christianity; and, Dr. John S. Mbiti, author of *Introduction to African Religions*, which describes African religions within a broad and historically cultural heritage, including historical Christianity. Mbiti validates Anyike's thesis by describing Christianity as a "indigenous, traditional and African religion."

James Anyike's reasons, in part, for writing this book from an African Christian heritage are supported by such documentation as Dr. Mbiti, one of the world's leading theologians and African historians. My hope is that brother Anyike will expand this book when he issues the next reprint. It will be interesting to see if other black Christian and non-Christian scholars will critically respond to Anyike's premises. Anyike is a young black scholar to be reckoned with by friend and opponent. In this book one sees clearly the historical roots of Christianity as it evolved from Old Testament Judaism into and through New Testament Judaism. Anyike locates the death and resurrection of Jesus the Christ, and the radical leadership of his disciples at Pentecost and Antioch, as the earliest seminal development of Christianity.

African people of the continent, and those scattered across the diaspora, need the best weapons possible in order to once again take their places as spiritual leaders on this planet. This book is one more necessary weapon in this spiritual and historical arsenal.

May the God of our Ancestors and of our African-Biblical faith continue to inspire younger warrior-scholars, such as James Chikaodili Anyike. His works must be promoted nationally as paradigms and examples for thousands of other young black men and women whose lives seem to be centered around everything else, other than historically African centered revolutionary Christianity.

Dr. Kwame John R. Porter, Ph.D, Pastor
Christ United Methodist Pan-African Pentecostal Fellowship
Chicago, IL

INTRODUCTION

Most people throughout the world have been affected in one way or another by the existence of Christianity. After nearly 2000 years, it's similar to a mighty tree with millions of leaves, thousands of branches and hundreds of stems all connecting to one common stem called the "trunk." Likewise, Christianity is represented by millions of people who belong to thousands of denominations of hundreds of religious organizations, all originating with one common biblical figure called "Jesus Christ."

The racism prevalent today in many parts of the world did not exist during Bible times (about 3000 B.C. to 1 A.D.). Neither was racism a major factor as the Christian church developed from the 1st to the 6th centuries. The Bible gives no clear indication that race mattered among biblical people as a religious, economic, social or political factor. However, racism was imposed on Christianity, and resulted in the belief that biblical people were white.

The physical appearance of Jesus is popularly perceived as very Caucasian. This perception also applies to most biblical figures. For many Christians, the acceptance of biblical figures as white is hardly questioned. However, challenges to these false portrayals have escalated as more non-whites research the historical, anthropological, archaeological, genetic and theological facts.

It is inconsistent for Christians to represent the gospel (means "good news") as a gospel of truth, and yet not challenge lies told about the "Savior" that the religion represents. If biblical figures in their true ethnic appearance become unacceptable to Christians because they were black people,

1

then the believers' racism becomes more powerful then their faith and submission to God. One of the earliest known portraits of Jesus is found in the Catacomb of Dormitilla in Rome. This 2nd century portrayal is that of a very dark skinned man with black hair. In Chapter 6, this matter is dealt with in detail.

The same false perceptions exist about the founding of Christianity. The popular perception is that a white Jesus was crucified and died, was resurrected on the third day, gave a command to his white disciples to spread the gospel, and made white Paul an apostle to the Romans. The biblical record places a great deal of emphasis on the writings and ministries involving Rome and Asia Minor. These canonical scriptures say nothing about the thriving growth of Christianity in Alexandria, Egypt, which may have started as early as 39 A.D.

It has been impressed upon us that the religion started with a small group of persecuted Jews, but was nurtured and spread when the Roman government accepted it under Constantine. An accurate history of early Christianity cannot be presented without inclusion of the African contributions to the religion.

An accurate historian will not hesitate to acknowledge that the Kemites (Egyptians) of Bible times were black people; that the most highly respected of the church fathers were African men; that Christian monasticism was started by an African man; that the first Christian educational institution was started by an African; that African church leaders were at the forefront of every major ecumenical council during the first five centuries of the religion; and that Africans served a most crucial role as translators and preservers of the biblical scriptures.

Through this text, the historical record of early Christianity is made clear and inclusive of the African cultures that contributed to it. The information provided herein is not slanted to create false impressions and myths about the roles of black people in early Christianity. *Historical Christianity African Centered* is presented as a missing link in popular Christian history and seeks to enhance the presentation of Christianity with its rich African heritage.

This text has four major parts. In Part 1 the racial composition of the Israelites and other Old Testament people is explored.

Chapter 1, The Sons of Noah, examines the close relationships between those considered the descendants of Ham and Shem. Through our examination of the families of Noah's three sons, we will identify the close cultural and racial similarities between people classified as "Semitic" and those classified as "Hamitic."

Chapter 2, The Children of Father Abraham, examines the interaction that Abraham and his descendants had with different people from Mesopotamia to Kemit. It is interesting to note that Abraham came from an ancient city of the Mesopotamia called Ur, which was a region of black people. This chapter also presents an examination of the intermixing that took place between Abraham's family and black Semitic and Hamitic people.

Chapter 3, Israel Becoming an Egyptian People, explores the making of Israel into a Kemitic (Egyptian) people in culture, language and race. A small group of about 70 members of Joseph's family joined him in Egypt, and in less then 400 years the children of Israel multiplied to more than 600,000 men of military age. Adding children, women and elders would probably increase the total to more than two million people during the exodus period. This growth must have involved intermixing with the Kemites. With more than 99.9 percent of the Israelites first four generations being born in Kemit, they were a Kemitic people when they left Kemit.

Chapter 4, Israel Scattered Among the Nations, provides an overview of Israel's interaction with different nations from the exodus period to the time of Persian domination. Despite the laws against intermixing with people that worshipped other gods, many of the children of Israel continued to intermix. Weakened through wars and internal conflicts, the tribes of Judah and Benjamin split from the other 10 tribes in 922 B.C., producing a separate "Jewish" kingdom from Israel. In 721 B.C., Israel was conquered by the Assyrians. Samaria, the capital of Israel, became a place of idolatry and mixed heritage. The Jews were subject to further foreign rule under the Babylonians and Persians. The children of Israel were a shadow of their past greatness when Alexander conquered Palestine in 332 B.C.

Chapter 5, Greek and Roman Rule over Israel, presents a historical picture of Palestine from 332 B.C. to 1 A.D. This examination of Greek and Roman rule in the Mediterranean region explains the political and social relationships they had with Israel. In this chapter, the Maccabean and Herodian dynasties are introduced, setting the stage for the political climate that existed during the birth of Christianity.

In Part 2 the history of the New Testament is introduced, with a special emphasis on the race of Jesus, the disciple, apostles and early proselytes.

4

Chapter 6, The Biblical and Historical Jesus, presents a wide range of sources to show how Jesus was portrayed and perceived in early history. The biblical Jesus was a young revolutionary. The earliest portrayals of Jesus were of a black man. Such portrayals are found in Roman catacombs, a Roman coin with Jesus on one side and Caesar on the other, and hundreds of statues and paintings of Jesus and Mary, popularly called the "Madonna and child."

Chapter 7, Jesus' Disciples and Apostles, is a general introduction to the hundreds of people called disciples of Jesus and brief biographies of the 12 disciples and apostles that were closest to him. This chapter also presents a historical review of the spreading of Christianity throughout the first century. During the 1st century there were many conflicts among early Christians and controversies about Gentiles (Europeans) joining the religion and whether they were subject to Jewish laws. The New Testament pays little attention to the efforts of the original apostles of Jesus in spreading the gospel. Most of the emphasis is on the works and writings of Paul. It is interesting to note that Paul had the physical appearance of an "Egyptian," according to the 21st chapter of Acts in the Bible. This chapter highlights the efforts to spread the gospel to the black people of the Mediterranean region and the persecuting of Christians by the Roman government.

Chapter 8, 1st Century Christianity in Africa, gives special emphasis to what became the strongest community of early Christianity. Because the first apostles were Jews, they placed most of their emphasis on converting Jews. There were many Jewish communities outside of Judea. The community of Jews in Alexandria, Egypt, was the largest of the diaspora. Because

5

Alexandria was only 380 miles from Jerusalem, travel between the two cities was common. It is not likely that the apostles would fail to spread the gospel to Alexandria. According to Coptic tradition, St. Mark journeyed to Egypt to establish a community of Christians.

In Part 3, the important contributions of Africa to early Christianity are presented. Their impact on the religion is invaluable. The lack of attention given to this subject by church historians is nothing less than racist and reprehensible.

Chapter 9, Christian and Egyptian Beliefs Compared, compares the ancient Kemitic myth of Osiris to the biblical Jesus Christ. The myth of Osiris may be more than 10,000 years old and many of the attributes ascribed to Jesus Christ were first represented in the myths about Osiris.

Chapter 10, Fathers of the Christian Church, gives credit to these African men who are held in high esteem in Christian history, but are seldom referred to as "black" or "African" people. Highly respected are Tertullian as the creator of Christian Latin literature; Cyprian as the source of the Episcopalian and papalist views of church order; Origin as an interpreter of orthodoxy, educator and profound writer; and Augustine as a theologian, defender of Christianity and Bishop of Hippo.

Chapter 11, Christian Education, informs the reader about the first theological institution of Christianity, which is called the *Didascalia* or *Catechetical School of Alexandria*. It provided the highest training in Christian thought during the third and fourth centuries. Prominent African heads of the school included Clement and Origin. It was at the Didascalia that many profound theological ideas were developed and documented.

Chapter 12, Christian Monasticism, is an introduction and tribute to the founders of Christian monasticism, which began in Egypt in the third century. The three people most responsible for establishing monasticism are St. Antony, St. Pachomius and Mary.

Chapter 13, Preservers of the Scriptures, discusses how the first translations of the Old and New Testaments were made in Kemit. Thanks to African monasteries, many biblical writings were hidden from Roman officials who sought to destroy them. They also preserved writings that were declared heretical. Throughout the last century, many ancient manuscripts have been found in Egypt. The most significant find was in 1945 near Nag Hammadi in Upper Egypt.

Chapter 14, African Martyrs, examines the zeal of African Christians that considered it a great honor to die for their faith in Jesus Christ. Most inspiring are the reports of bravery and miracles among the martyrs. The persecution of Christians lasted almost 400 years throughout the Roman Empire.

Throughout Part 4, a brief history of Christianity after the Council of Chalcedon is presented. The focus of the religion shifted from Africa to Rome, largely due to military and political force.

Chapter 15, Coptic and Catholic Split, provides brief histories of these two churches after they split. Special emphasis is given to the Coptic church history.

Chapter 16, How Christianity was Colored White, shows how history was distorted to produce the false perception that the people of the Bible were white. In 1508 Pope Julius II commissioned Michelangelo to paint a portrait of Jesus. White images of the biblical figures created by Michelangelo have become popularly accepted as historically accurate. Motion pictures about biblical events have instilled indelible mental images in our minds that Moses looked like Charlton Heston (an American actor) and spoke an old English dialect. We challenge the use of these false images that have been used to support white supremacy.

Chapter 17, Christians Reclaiming Africentrism, is a challenge to Christians to accept the truth about African contributions to Christianity. For more than 1,500 years black Christians have accepted false white portrayals of biblical figures. Can white Christians accept true black portrayals of biblical figures and are they prepared to receive a black Jesus when he returns (the return of Jesus is expected by most Christians)?

It is likely that this information will be considered racist by many people. This text is not a replacement of white racism, with black racism. Before this work is judged negatively, one important question must be answered: "Is this a truthful and accurate portrayal of history based on historical, biblical, and archaeological facts?" If the answer is "no," then it must be objectively challenged in order to produce a more historically accurate report. If the answer is "yes," it must be accepted and given respect, as the truth deserves. It is a confirmation of the old sayings, "Truth crushed to earth will rise again" and "The truth will make you free."

8

CHAPTER 1

THE SONS OF NOAH

The book of Genesis (the first book of the Bible) reports that Noah was commanded by God to build an ark that would be used to save the earth's animals and Noah's family from a flood. The people who entered the ark were Noah, his wife (whose name is not given in the Bible), his three sons Japheth, Shem and Ham, and his son's wives, whose names are not given.

Accordingly, these were the people who survived the flood and fruitfully multiplied to replenish the earth. The race of Noah's family is not stated in the Bible. Yet, a biblical and historical study of those people who are identified as descendants of Noah's sons will lead to a firm conclusion about their race.

The focus of this chapter is on Shem and his descendants, leading up to Abraham in about 1800 B.C. It is from Shem that the children of Israel come to be. There are four terms that must be defined to give us a better understanding of who we are talking about. The terms are *Semite*, *Hebrew*, *Israel* and *Jews*. A Semite is any person who descended from Shem. A Hebrew is any descendant from Heber (also Eber), a great-grandson of Shem. The name Israel refers to Jacob, Abraham's grandson, and Jacob's descendants. Jews identifies members of the tribes of Judah and Benjamin jointly, which split from the other 10 tribes. According to the 11th chapter of Genesis, the survivors of the flood traveled east and settled in Shinar.

The Bible reports that the ark rested on Mount Ararat. For hundreds of years there have been many reported sightings of

Figure 1:
The Genealogy of Shem

<table>
<tr><td colspan="5" align="center">SHEM
(Semites)</td></tr>
</table>

ELAM (Elamites)	ASSHUR (Assyrians)	ARPHAXAD	LUD	ARAM (Syrians)
		SALAH		
		HEBER (Hebrews)		

PELEG	JOKTAN
REU	14 Sons
SERUG	
NAHOR	
TERAH	

NAHOR	ABRAHAM	HARAN

This genealogy shows that the Elamites, Assyrians, Syrians and Hebrews were all Semitic people, as descendants of Shem. All of the descendants of Heber are identified as "Hebrews."

10

the ark on Mount Ararat.(1)

Before they traveled east, we learn from the 9th chapter of Genesis about Noah planting a vineyard, getting drunk from wine and falling asleep naked. Ham, Noah's youngest son, found his father in this condition and reported it to his brothers. Subsequently, Noah was angry with Ham and cursed Canaan, Ham's son. The reason for his anger is not clear, nor is it clear why Canaan was targeted rather than Ham and/or all of his sons. Furthermore, whether Noah had authority from God to curse anyone in his hungover condition is highly questionable.

Some historians and theologians have used this story to justify enslaving black people. Those who supported slavery argued that the proper station in life for blacks was to be hewers of wood, drawers of water and servants to the white race. It is interesting to note that this racist explanation of the curse concedes that the Canaanites are black people. The Israelites often intermixed with the Canaanites, as will be proven in the following chapters.

Even more puzzling is the story of the Tower of Babel in the 11th chapter of Genesis. From this story we learn that some time after they settled in Shinar, God "came down to see the city and tower" the people built. God became displeased with their abilities of communication and imagination. For this reason God "confounded" their language so they could not understand each other and "scattered" them across the earth.

These stories may be symbolic representations of how people were spread throughout the world. The author has no intentions to prove or disprove the veracity of these stories. The reader may choose to view them as historical, biblical or

11

mythical accounts of how the earth was replenished and how people were scattered throughout the world. They are used herein to provide biblical references to the more historically verifiable accounts of the existence of the Jews, which led to the establishing of Christianity.

After the "scattering," the descendants of Japheth are seldom referred to in the Bible. The children of Ham and Shem had practically no interaction with their Japhethite relatives.

Shem was the second born of Noah's sons and the ancestor of the Semitic people. He had five sons and three of these are the ancestors of tribes with identified geographical locations.(2) Elam produced the Elamites, Asshur produced the Assyrians and Aram produced the Arameans (also called Syrians). Shem's son Arphaxad was the grandfather of Heber. It is from Heber that the Hebrew tribe is produced. No geographical location is identified for this tribe.

For many years historians used three classifications to group the people of the earth according to similarities in language, religion and appearance. The classifications were Hamitic, Semitic and Japhetic.(3) In general, the Hamitic people were regarded as black Africans (or Negroid); the Semitic people as Asian (or Mongoloid); and the Japhetic people as white Europeans (or Caucasoid).

Subsequently, the association of Hamitic people with blackness was changed to include white people. This was probably done by racist historians who could not accept the fact that the first and greatest civilizations (i.e. Egyptian and Mesopotamian) were black civilizations. Historians dis-associated Hamites from the so-called "Negroes" in western and southern Africa. Accordingly, the Kemites, Ethiopians and

Mesopotamians were described as "dark-skinned whites," "dark red," "copper colored," "brown," "whites with black skin," "Mediterranean," "Eurafrican" or "Caucasoid blacks."(4) However, it has been proven that the people of these great civilizations were basically the same as the rest of the people of the African continent, having dark (or black) skin, thick lips, broad noses and kinky black hair.(5)

The ancient Semites are closely associated with the Hamites in language, religious beliefs and most often in appearance. The Hebrew language is closely related to that of the Canaanites. Many philologists agree that there are definite connections between the Semitic and Hamitic languages, but neither closely connect to Aryan tongues. Historian H.G. Wells said, "The Semitic languages may have arisen as some specialized proto-Hamitic group."(6) Sumerian is the oldest written language known. This Hamitic tongue, used by the Mesopotamian civilization of Sumer more than 6,000 years ago, is used today by philologist as the foundation for the study of the development of languages.(7)

Like Hamitic people, the Semites also engaged in worship of the sun and fertility or phallus symbols. The ancient Hebrews also engaged in dice throwing, sacrificing to idols and worship of the sun god Bel. Terah, Abraham's father, and his contemporaries were known to "serve other gods."(8) The worship of idols seemed to come easy to the children of Israel after they left Egypt. The Bible reports that God was prepared to destroy them when they made a golden calf and began worshiping it. Aaron's excuse to his brother Moses for the idolatry was "thou knowest the people, that they are set on mischief."(9) Researcher Dr. Charles Finch III asserts that the

13

exodus of the Israelites from Egypt resulted from their worship of the god Set after worshipers of Amen gained power in Egypt.(10)

Geographically, the descendants of Shem are always found in lands with, or close to, Hamitic people, as was the case with the descendants of Elam living with the Sumerians. Approximately 180 miles north of the Persian Gulf was the ancient city of Susa, which was the capital of Elam. It was one of the earliest historic civilizations of high culture and sat on the eastern border of Sumer. It dates back to about 3000 B.C. and is often compared to the Nile Valley civilization of Egypt. The Elamites developed copper weapons, cultivated grain, domesticated animals and had hieroglyphic writings and business documents.(11)

Historical, archaeological and anthropological evidence verifies that these descendants of Elam, one of Shem's sons, were black. According to Egyptologist Gaston Maspero, the Elamites were "a short and robust people of well-knit figure with brown skin, black hair...who belong to the negritic race." English Orientalist George Rawlinson said the Elamites had a "negro type of countenance," that their heads were "covered with short crisp curls," and that they had "thick lips."(12) Further proof of the black heritage of Elam is provided through the efforts of archaeologist Marcel Auguste Dieulafoy, who found depictions of black rulers on panels of enamelled bricks from ancient Susa, the capital of Elam.(13)

About 380 miles northwest of Susa was the land of Assyria. Its major cities included Asshur and Nimrud and its founders were migrants from Babylon. Genesis identifies Ham's son, Nimrod, as its founder.(14) The Assyrians are well known for being the first to equip its large army with iron weapons, and ultimately became an empire dominating Babylon, Palestine, Egypt, and most of the Near East.

The early history of Assyria dates back to about 2300 B.C. According to Egyptologist Jean Francois Champollion, examination of bas-reliefs on the tomb of Sesostris I depict images of Asians represented differently from those of the Egyptian and European images. The Assyrian image is described as having "tanned complexion, aquiline nose, black eyes and thick beard...clad in rare splendor."(15) A 7th century Assyrian relief from the palace of Ashurbanipal shows Assyrian musicians with broad noses, thick lips, heavy beards and dread locks (or a head piece that looks like dreadlocks).(16)

Syria was located about 355 miles west and slightly south of Nineveh, and about 50 miles east of The Great Sea (later called the Mediterranean Sea). The depictions of Syrians found in Egyptian bas-reliefs and wall paintings show them with very dark skin with unmistakenly African-type features. A 13th century B.C. painting, which is part of a decoration at the base of the throne of Amenhotep III, shows two Syrians with black hair, thick lips, broad noses and dark skin.(17) Other images of black Syrians are found on the ceremonial walking stick of Tut-ankh-Amon, the tomb of Horemheb at Memphis, the tomb of Amenemheb at Thebes and a painting of a Syrian warrior from Tell el-Amarna.

The fact that Semitic and Hamitic people were neighbors produced strong relations between them. At times they engaged in trade, intermixing and war. Based on the archaeological and historical information presented about the Elamites, Assyrians and Syrians, we can conclude that they were not white. On the contrary, they were basically black people. The lack of proof supporting a Caucasian presence among these people further justifies this position. If it is true that the descendants of Shem's three sons were black, then their patriarchs were black. This gives us good reason to conclude that Shem and his other two sons were black.

NOTES

1) LaHaye, Tim and John Morris, *The Ark on Ararat,* (Thomas Nelson Inc., Publishers, New York, NY 1976).
2) See figure one on page 10.
3) McCray, Rev. Walter Arthur, *The Black Presence in the Bible,* (Black Light Fellowship, Chicago, IL 1990) p. 41 and Wells, H.G., *The Outline of History,* (The MacMillan Company, New York, NY 1921) p. 110.
4) Diop, Cheikh Anta, *The African Origin of Civilization,* (Lawrence Hill & Company, Westport, 1974) Chapter 3.
5) Dunston, Bishop Alfred G. Jr., *The Black Man in the Old Testament and its World,* (Africa World Press, Inc., Trenton, NJ 1992).
6) Wells, *The Outline of History,* p. 121.
7) *Insight Magazine,* "Tracking Mother of 5000 Tongues" by Harvey Hagman, February 5, 1990, pp. 54-55.
8) *The African Heritage Study Bible,* King James Version (The James C. Winston Publishing Company, Nashville, TN 1993) Joshua 24:2.
9) Ibid., Exodus 32:22.
10) Van Sertima, Ivan and Runoko Rashidi, Editors, *African Presence in Early Asia,* (Transaction Books, New Brunswick, GA 1988) pp. 190-192.
11) Durant, Will, *Our Oriental Heritage,* (Simon and Schuster, New York, 1954) p. 117.
12) Van Sertima, *African Presence in Early Asia,* p. 20.
13) Diop, *The African Origin of Civilization,* pp. 103-104.
14) *The African Heritage Study Bible,* Genesis 10:11.

15) Diop, *The African Origin of Civilization,* p. 47.
16) Comay, Joan and Ronald Brownrigg, *Who's Who in the Bible,* (Bonanza Books, New York, NY 1980) p. 59.
17) Pritchard, James B., *The Ancient Near East in Pictures,* (Princeton University Press, Princeton, NJ 1954) p. 2.

CHAPTER 2

THE CHILDREN OF FATHER ABRAHAM

This examination of Abraham and his descendants will present scriptural and historical information to show how they had very close relationships with Hamitic people. In fact, they had more contact with Hamitic people than Semitic people. The integration of Abraham and his descendants with Hamitic people was by choice, in some cases, and commanded by God in others. When Abraham's family is first introduced in the 11th chapter of Genesis, they were living among Hamites in Ur of the Chaldees.

Acceptance of the belief that the biblical Hamites were black people is most important in concluding that the early Hebrews were greatly influenced by a distinctly black people. In general, Hamites are classified as black, despite the efforts of some historians to classify them as white.(1) Fortunately, the weight of historical and archaeological proof remains on the side of those who support belief in Hamitic blackness, as will be shown in this chapter.

At this point, it is crucial that we identify the Hamites of the Bible and present references that validate their blackness. Ham, the youngest son of Noah, had four sons. Their names were Cush, Egypt, Put (or Phut) and Canaan. The genealogies of Ham's sons are provided in Figure 1 and show what nations were produced from them.

According to Old Testament scholar Charles B. Copher, "The evidences indicate that, in the main, wherever in the Bible Hamites are referred to they were people who, today in the

Figure 1:
The Genealogies of Ham's Sons

CUSH
(Cushites or Ethiopians)

SEBA RAAMAH HAVILAH SABTECHAN NIMROD SABTAH
_____(Traditional Founder
SHEBA   DEDAN   of Babel, Erech, Accad,
                                          Calneh, Asshur, Nineveh,
                                          Rehoboth and Calah.)

EGYPT or MIZRAIM
(Egyptians or Kemites)

ANAMIM LUDIM LEHABIM CASLUHIM NAPHTUHIM CAPHTORIM PATHRUSIM
(Philistines)

CANAAN
(The Canaanites included the Jebusites, Amorites, Girgasites, Hivites,
Arkites, Sinites, Arvadites, Zamarites, Phoenicians and Hamathites.)

SIDON or ZIDON   HETH
                                (Hittites)

PHUT
(The traditional ancestor of the Libyans or Cyrenes, no descendants
are listed in the Bible.)

According to the Bible, the sons of Ham were Cush, Egypt, Canaan and
Phut. These sons and their descendants are classified as "Hamites."

Western world, would be classified as Black, and Negroid."(2) There is much evidence to support the black heritage of those Hamites of the African continent and Mesopotamian region.

The United Nations Educational, Scientific and Cultural Organization (UNESCO) reached a consensus at its Cairo Symposium in 1974, which stated "There is no evidence that the ancient Egyptians were white, and that Egypt was not influenced by Mesopotamia, but by peoples from the Great Lakes region in inner-equatorial Africa." George Rawlinson confirms that "the fundamental character of the Egyptian in respect of physical type, language and tone of thought, is Nigritic."(3)

The blackness of the Cushites is generally accepted with little disagreement. Tribes identified as descendants of Cush are mostly located in Africa and Arabia.(4) African Cushites occupied the regions that are now known as Sudan, Ethiopia and Somalia. The names of these regions "speak for themselves" in verifying their black heritage. The name "Sudan" means "land of the blacks" and "Ethiopia" literally means "land of burnt faces."

Nimrod, one of the sons of Cush, is addressed in the Bible as "a mighty one in the earth" and "a mighty hunter before the lord." He is also identified as the founder of many of the nations in the Mesopotamian region (Genesis 10:8-12). According to Rev. Walter A. McCray, author of *The Black Presence in the Bible,* "There are also definite linguistic relationships between Cush, Kish, Cassites (Kassites), and Cosseans. Furthermore, the 'Cush' of this passage is related also to Assyria via Babylonia, Cushite civilization advanced up the Tigris-Euphrates."(5)

21

The Canaanites and the Phoenicians are one and the same. These Hamitic people are said to have "dwelt" in Canaan "of old," according to 1st Chronicles 4:40. They were a peaceful people who inhabited the "land that floweth with milk and honey," which was promised to the children of Israel, according to the Bible. Since ancient times they were believed to be the inventors of navigation. Cheikh Anta Diop described the Phoenicians as "a Negroid people, more or less cousins of the Egyptians."(6)

The process of identifying the Putites as black people is less obvious than other Hamitic people. Though no genealogy is given in the Bible for Put, the Libyans are traditionally recognized as his descendants. Flavius Josephus identifies Put as the founder of Libya. Historically, the difficulty in the identification process results from the invasion of the Western region of the Nile Delta by tall, blond, blue-eyed Indo-Europeans around 1500 B.C.(7) According to Dr. Jacob Curruthers of the Association for the Study of Classical African Civilization (ASCAC), northern Libya was occupied by white people that the ancient Egyptians called "Tchemehu." The Egyptians distinguished them from the black people (who looked like them) of southern Libya called "Tchehenu." A 12th century B.C. Egyptian glazed tile shows a distinctly black Libyan (see page 38). The presence of white Libyans in the region led some historians to believe northern Africa was generally inhabited by a white indigenous population. However, they were Indo-European invaders (or migrants), and not a Putite people like the black Libyans.

The question that should be asked at this point is "what contact did Abram (Abraham) and his descendants have with

22

these black people?" Abram and his family started their journey from Ur of the Chaldeans, a region of black people that may have been politically dominated by the Cassites (possibly a Cushite people), around 2100 B.C.

According to the 11th chapter of Genesis, Terah took his son Abram, his grandson Lot, and Abram's wife Sarai (also Terah's daughter) to go into the land of Canaan. They traveled along the Fertile Crescent, northeast to Haran. Before going south to Canaan, they settled in Haran where they had a home, amassed "substance" (or material wealth), and bought (or hired) servants. Haran was a commercial center in the northern region of Assyria and probably was a place where different nationalities lived. While living there, Terah died.

In chapter 12 of Genesis, Abram is told by "the Lord" to leave "his fathers house (in Haran) unto a land that I will shew thee" where "I will make thee a great nation, and I will bless thee. ...And I will bless them that bless thee, and curse him that curseth thee." This "promised land" was Canaan, a land inhabited by Hamitic people. They set up a tent in the mountains between Bethel and Hai (or Ai), but soon traveled to Egypt because there was a famine in Canaan.

While in Egypt, Abram introduced Sarai as his sister (she was his half-sister, born of a different mother). Though she was about 65 years old, she was described as appealing to the Egyptians and Abram allowed her to be taken into Pharaoh's house. In return, he was given much livestock and many servants. It is strongly implied that Pharaoh and Sarai had sexual relations. This is the first sexual encounter between a Hebrew and Hamite that was reported in the Bible. If there was no sexual activity, there would have been no reason for God to strike Pharaoh's house with a plague.

After leaving Egypt they traveled south (probably to Cush). They then traveled back to Bethel after becoming very rich in silver, gold and cattle. A dispute arose among the Hamitic herdsmen of Lot and Abram. These men were Perizzites and Canaanites. Abram suggested that they separate into different regions so they could live without conflict. Abram remained in Canaan and Lot moved to Sodom.

The location of Sodom and the other cities that shared the region (Gomorrah, Admah, Zeboiim and Zoar) is not known for certain. The five countries were a part of a federation called "the Vale of Siddim" and was probably located along the southeast shore of the Salt Sea (later called the Dead Sea). The region was subject to Elamite rule and rebelled against the king of Elam named Chedorlaomer. Sodom was probably a Semitic country because it was subject to black Semitic authority in Elam.

The rebellious actions of the Vale of Siddim led to an attack on them by Chedorlaomer and three other kingdoms, which were victorious in ransacking Sodom. Lot was taken captive, which caused Abram to get involved to rescue his nephew. He took 300 men (servants) from his house to defeat Chedorlaomer's forces and rescue Lot. Most of the men with Abram were Hamites. Aside from a few servants who may have joined him in Haran, the rest were Egyptians, Cushites and Canaanites. It is important to note that Abram and Sarai have lived only in Hamite lands after leaving Haran. Therefore, most of their servants naturally would be Hamitic. Abram also received help from three Amorite brothers named Memre, Eshcol and Aner. This is the first biblical report of Hamites and Hebrews joining as allies in war.

After the conflict was over, Abram was met in the Valley of Sheveh by Melchizedek, the Priest/King of Salem (later called Jerusalem). He was the ruler of the Jebusites, a Canaanite people, and he is referred to in the Bible as "the priest of the most high God." The same order of high priest that Jesus is identified with in the book of Hebrews (chapter 7, verses 1-3). Melchizedek bought bread and wine with him when he came to bless Abram. From Abram, he received a tithe (10 percent) of all that he had. It is interesting to note the presence of these Christian symbols (bread, wine and tithe) in the time of Abram and their use by a Hamite priest.

After living among the Canaanites for 10 years, Abram was encouraged by Sarai to produce a child with Hagar, her Egyptian handmaid. Abram expressed no apprehensions about having sexual relations and producing a child with an Egyptian. From this relationship came Ishmael. At this time Abram was 86 years old. Ishmael is traditionally considered the ancestor of the Arabic people.

At the age of 99 Abram received a message from God changing his name to "Abraham" and his wife's name to "Sarah." Abraham was also given instructions to accept the African practice of circumcision. According to Herodotus "the Egyptians and Ethiopians are the only nations who practiced circumcision from the earliest times."

The Dogon (Sudanese) practiced circumcision and excision of their children to assure proper sexual inclination of the children during puberty. Like the Egyptians, they believed that the first god ("Amma" in Dogon and "Amen" in Egypt) was naturally androgynous and that this characteristic was passed

25

on to new born babies. Therefore, the foreskin of the male penis was considered a female element, and the clitoris of the female vagina was considered a male element. The foreskin and clitoris were cut away to incline males toward full masculinity and females towards full femininity.(8)

According to the Bible, Abraham was given this practice as a covenant with God (Genesis 17:11). However, Diop believed Abraham's relationship with Hagar may have influenced the introduction of this practice. This is consistent with the words of the ancient geographer Strabo, who wrote in his *Geographical*:

> The Egyptians are especially careful in raising all their children and circumcise the boys and even the girls, a custom common to the Jews, a people originally from Egypt. (Book 17, chap.1, par.29)

In Chapter 3 attention will be given to the belief that the Israelites were a people originally from Egypt.

The genealogy of Abraham clearly shows that his descendants were not pure Hebrew. They were either Hebrew-Syrian, Hebrew-Egyptian or Hebrew-Canaanite.

Even if Abraham and Sarah were pure Europeans (with blonde hair, blue eyes and white skin), their descendants would have lost their white appearance and culture through years of integration and miscegenation. Abraham had six children and five of them were Egyptians. Of his 21 grandchildren, 19 were Egyptians.

Figure 2:
The Genealogies of Abraham

ABRAHAM & HAGAR

ISHMAEL
(Ishmaelites)

NEBOJOTH	KEDAR	ADBAAL	MIDSAM	MISHMA	DUMAH	MASSA
	HADAR	TEMA	JETUR	NAPHISM	KEDAMAH	

ABRAHAM & KETURAH

JOKSHAN	MEDAN	ZIMRAN	MIDIAN
			(Midianites)

SHEBA	DEDAN

EPHAH EPHER HANOCH ABIDAH ELDAAH

ABRAHAM & SARAH

ISAAC
(Isaac's Genealogy provided in Figure 3)

Both Hagar and Keturah were Egyptian wives of Abraham.

27

Figure 3:
The Genealogy of Isaac

ISAAC & REBEKAH

ESAU	JACOB/ISRAEL
(Had 5 sons through 3 Canaanite wives Aholibamah, Adah, & Bashmath)	FATHER OF THE 12 TRIBES (See below)

JEUSH JAALAM KORAH ELIPHAZ REUEL

JACOB & LEAH

REUBEN SIMEON LEVI JUDAH ISSACHAR ZEBULIN DINAH

JACOB & RACHEL   JACOB & ZILPAH

JOSEPH   BENJAMIN   GAD   ASHER

JACOB & BILHAH

DAN   NAPHTALI

Jacob's wives, Leah and Rachel, were Syrian and their handmaids, Zilpah and Bilhah, were most likely Syrian or Egyptian.

His son, Isaac, married a Syrian woman. The Syrians were depicted as black people in ancient bas-reliefs and paintings.(9) Isaac married Rebekah, the daughter of Bethuel "the Syrian."(10) Abraham arranged their marriage, insisting that his son must marry a relative from his original home in the Mesopotamian region. Rebekah was Isaac's cousin and the great-granddaughter of Nahor, Abraham's brother. Abraham specifically stated that Isaac must not marry a Canaanite.

Isaac and Rebekah had twin sons, Esau and Jacob. Esau grieved his parents when he took three Hittite women as wives (Genesis 26:35). Nevertheless, Isaac intended to bless Esau as his heir, regardless of his Canaanite wives. However, this blessing went to Jacob, who conspired with Rebekah and tricked Isaac into giving the blessing to Jacob.

Jacob, like his father and grandfather, married within his family. Isaac sent him to Laban, Rebekah's brother, to choose a wife of his daughters. Jacob arranged to serve Laban for seven years in exchange for taking Rachel, Laban's youngest daughter, as his wife. After the seven years Laban tricked him by giving him Leah, his oldest daughter, instead of Rachel. Jacob served him for seven more years to receive Rachel as his wife.

Rachel and Leah, like their aunt Rebekah, were Syrian. Both women had handmaids. Zilpah was a handmaid to Leah, and Bilhah was Rachel's handmaid. These women were most likely Egyptian or Syrian, considering Isaac's instructions for Jacob to not mix with any Canaanites. Like Sarah and Rebekah, Jacob's two wives experienced periods of barrenness. During these periods, their handmaids were used to produce children for Jacob.

29

Through these Syrian wives and their handmaids, Jacob gave birth to the 12 tribes of Israel.(11) These were not white women. The biblical Syrians and Egyptians were black people. The least that can be said about the children of Israel is they were a mixed Hebrew-Syrian and/or Hebrew-Egyptian people. However, this mixed heritage will end as the children of Israel become completely Egyptian, as is explained in the next chapter.

NOTES

1) Copher, Charles B. *Black Biblical Studies,* (Black Light Fellowship, Chicago, IL 1990) p. 123.
2) Ibid., p. 36.
3) Ibid., p. 29.
4) McCray, Rev. Walter Arthur. *The Black Presence in the Bible Vol.2,* (Black Light Fellowship, Chicago, IL 1990) p. 95.
5) Ibid., p. 96.
6) Diop, Cheikh Anta. *The African Origin of Civilization,* (Lawrence Hill & Company, Westport, 1974) p. 166.
7) Diop, Cheikh Anta. *The Cultural Unity of Black Africa,* (Third World Press, Chicago, IL 1978) pp. 62-63.
8) Diop, *The African Origin of Civilization,* pp. 136-137.
9) Chapter 1, p. 15.
10) *The Original African Study Bible,* King James Version, (James C. Winston Publishing Company, Nashville, TN 1993) Genesis 25:20.
11) Ibid., Genesis 29-30.

The following are illustrations of ancient images of various people of the Bible. Notice their black features.

Figure 1. A Elamite as depicted in an Egyptian bas-relief.

Figure 2. A Canaanite fertility goddess.

Figure 3. A Canaanite traveler as depicted in an Egyptian bas-relief.

Figure 4. An Egyptian hairdresser.

Figure 5. A Syrian as depicted on the ceremonial walking stick of Tut-Ankh-Amon.

Figure 6. A Assyrian musician with a dread lock hair style.

Figure 7. A Libya as depicted on an Egyptian glazed tile.

(Ilustrations by James C. Anyike)

Figure 1. ELAMITE

Figure 2. CANAANITE GODDESS

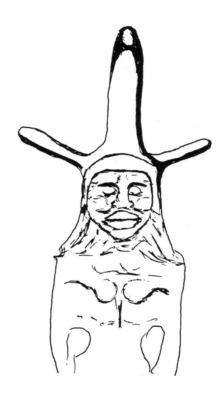

Figure 3. CANAANITE

Figure 4. EGYPTIAN

Figure 5. SYRIAN

Figure 6. ASSYRIAN

Figure 7. LIBYAN

CHAPTER 3

ISRAEL BECOMING AN EGYPTIAN PEOPLE

From the Bible we learn, in Chapter 37 of Genesis, that the jealousy and hatred felt by Joseph's older brothers was so great that they threw him into a pit and later sold him as a slave to some Ishmaelites. The Ishmaelites took Joseph to Egypt and sold him to Potipher, one of Pharaoh's officers and captain of the guard. After many tribulations and blessings, Joseph ultimately rose from slavery to rulership in 13 years. At the age of 30 Joseph was given power to govern the resources of all the land of Egypt.

Pharaoh gave Joseph the name "Zephnathpaaneah," which means "says the god, he will live." He was also given an Egyptian wife named Asenath. Together they had two sons, Manasseh and Ephraim. Joseph was later reunited with his family and forgave his brothers for the evil they did to him. Joseph made provisions for his family to live in Egypt, in the land of Goshen. According to Genesis 46:27, 70 members of the house of Jacob entered Egypt. The 70 included Jacob, his 12 sons, 51 grandsons, four great-grandsons, one daughter and one granddaughter. If we assume that all of his sons had one wife and half of his grandsons had wives, the total increases to 107 people.

Understanding the political atmosphere of Egypt is important to the argument that the children of Israel became an Egyptian people. It is believed that the Israelites entered Egypt around 1706 B.C., most likely after the Hyksos gained control of Egypt around 1783.(1) According to Manetho, a third century Egyptian priest, the Hyksos were "invaders of obscure race...from regions of the east" and "men of ignoble birth."(2) Some historians believe that the Hyksos were white invaders from Asia. Therefore, the argument has been made that the children of Israel mixed with Asiatic Hyksos, instead of black Egyptians.

There are several historical facts that verify a relationship between the Hyksos and Israelites. However, little evidence exists to prove that they were white or Indo-European invaders from Asia. The children of Israel were shepherds. The name "Hyksos" is interpreted to mean "chieftains of the hill country" or "shepherd kings." If this name is an indication that the Hyksos were a rural and nomadic people, unlike the urban citizens of Egypt, they shared this lower cast status with the Israelites. According to Genesis 46:34, the Israelites were given living space in Goshen because they were shepherds and "every shepherd is an abomination unto the Egyptians."

Martin Bernal writes, in *Black Athena*:

Apart from a general suggestion of a connection by the fact that the majority of Hyksos were, like the later Israelites, West Semitic speakers from Canaan, there are two specific reasons for supposing a more direct relationship. Firstly, there is the attestation in both Palestine and Lower Egypt of the name Ykb hr or Ykb as a Hyksos ruler in the late 18th century. This name is remarkably similar to Jacob, Ya aqov. Jacob Israel was not only the eponym and the specific ancestor of Israel, he was also the patriarch who, according to tradition, led the Israelites into Egypt, Secondly, there is the archaeological evidence from the fact that by far the highest density of Hyksos scarabs (an ornament representing a scarab beetle) is to be found in the territory now known as the West Bank, which at the end of the Bronze Age was the Israelite heartland.(3)

Considering the report of Manetho stating that the Hyksos were from "regions of the east," this may mean east in Egypt. Dr. Charles S. Finch III asserts "it could more logically and plausibly be assumed that he (Manetho) was referring to the shepherds and nomads of Egypt's eastern desert...."(4) He also states that "the pastoral people living in Egypt's eastern desert were, in effect, Egyptian nationals who clung to their traditional way of life and were a constant source of turbulence and unrest." Classifying the Hyksos as Egyptian aboriginals may be complicated by their being a Semitic-speaking people. However, there were 16 Semitic languages spoken among the Ethiopians, two of which were Gheez and Amharic. What's more, it is widely believed that Semitic languages grew out of Hamitic tongues. Bernal states that the "overwhelming majority of Hyksos in Egypt were Semitic-speaking and it is equally clear from names that, just as the material culture of the Hyksos at Tell el Dabaa became increasingly Egyptian in the 17th century B.C., the Egyptian language reasserted itself in the face of the Semitic."(5)

The race of the Hyksos cannot be identified with absolute certainty. However, Manetho reports that an 18th Dynasty Egyptian inscription stated that the Hyksos capital contained "Semitic speakers of Syro Palestine" with "wanderers" or "foreigners in their midst."(6) This implies that the Hyksos included a mix of people from regions of Syria and Palestine, and people foreign to them. These "foreigners" and "wanderers" may have been white people. According to Bernal, they were most likely non-Semitic speaking Hurrians or Indo-Iranian.

It is likely that the children of Israel were welcomed into Egypt by a Hyksos ruler, though no distinction is made in the Bible that identifies the Pharaoh as Hyksos. What's more, the Bible makes no mention of foreign rulers in Egypt when the Israelites entered with Jacob nor when they exited with Moses. Based upon this omission, an argument can be made in favor of Hyksos being convincing imitators of the Egyptian Pharaohs or actual Egyptians. These Hyksos Pharaohs of the Middle Kingdom (the 13th to the 17th Dynasties) lived as Egyptians and had Egyptian names. Gerald Massey, 19th century lecturer and author of the *Book of Beginnings,* took the position that the Hyksos were not foreigners in Egypt.(7) The political and cultural structures of Egypt remained unchanged under Hyksos rule.

The biblical Israelites were subject to Egyptian Pharaohs and lived among Egyptian people. These Israelites had Egyptian neighbors (Exodus 11:2 and 12:35). If there were other races and nations of people in Egypt, it is least likely that the Israelites would have intermixed with them. God did not put restrictions on their intermixing with Egyptians, as he did on their mixing with Canaanites. Neither God nor Jacob expressed any displeasure with Joseph having an Egyptian wife. In the 48th chapter of Genesis, Jacob proudly blessed Ephraim and Manasseh, the sons of Joseph and Asenath. These Egyptian men are the patriarchs of two of the Israelite tribes.

Around 1491 B.C., at the time of the exodus led by Moses, there were 603,550 men of fighting age among the Israelites. If we add women, elderly women, elderly men and children, the number of those that Moses led from Egypt would be more than two million. This very conservative estimate is based on at least 300,000 of these men having one wife, two parents and two children. The exact total in this case would be 1.5 million women, elders and children. When the 603,550 men are added to this total, we have more than 2.1 million people being led by Moses. Furthermore, this number does not include the "mixed multitude" that exited with them, as reported in Exodus 12:38. A more liberal estimate may be more than 3 million people.

According to Genesis 15:13-16, the Israelites' oppressors would "afflict them four hundred years" and "in the fourth generation, they shall come hither again." The fulfillment of this prophesy is provided in Exodus 12:40, which states "Now the sojourning of the children of Israel, who dwelt in Egypt, was four hundred and thirty years." How could the Israelites grow from 107 people to at least 2.1 million people in 400 years? The only realistic way that this increase could have happened is by their intermixing with the Egyptians.

Furthermore, all of the generations of the Israelites (four generations according to Genesis 15:16) lived most of their lives in Egypt. More than 99.9 percent of the pre-exodus Israelites were born in Egypt. The Israelites' ancestral ties began with Jacob Israel. His entire family migrated to Egypt and remained there for 430 years. Though they acknowledged their ethnic heritage as Israelites, they were Egyptian nationals.

The physical appearance of the Israelites was the same as the Egyptians. The earliest Israelites in Egypt were Hebrew Syrian and/or Hebrew-Egyptians.(8) After 430 years of living in the African climate and intermixing with the Egyptians, any physical variance would be genetically eliminated. Biblical proof for this position is established when the Midianite women refer to Moses as a "Egyptian" in Exodus 2:19. Midian was less than 150 miles from Egypt and the Midianites were descendants of Abraham and Keturah. These women knew what Egyptians looked like, and based on his appearance, they concluded that Moses was one.

There are names used in the Bible that specifically indicate the race of the individual. According to Rev. Walter A. McCray, "an example of identifying a Black personal name is 'Kedar' (very Black), or 'Phinehas' (the Negro, or the Nubian)."(9) The Kedarites were descendants of Ishmael. There are three people identified by the name "Phinehas" in the Bible. The first one was the grandson of Aaron. If the grandchild is black, it is likely that its parents and grandparents are black.

The Bible clearly confirms that the Israelites were not naturally white people. In the 13th chapter of Leviticus laws are established for the priest regarding leprosy. This form of leprosy caused a physical mutation to occur in some cases. This mutation involved the skin developing "bright" spots, scabs, white hair and other symptoms. In Leviticus 13:11-13, the priest may declare the person "clean" if all of the skin is "turned white" from head to foot, providing that no raw flesh is visible. If the skin of a person with white spots became "dark" after seven days, they were declared clean. The turning of the skin to white must have caused fascination and fear among the Israelites and Egyptians. When God instructed Moses to show Pharaoh his leprous hand (Genesis 4:7), it was meant to be a threat to Pharaoh. God also used leprosy to punish Mariam, Moses' sister, as recorded in Numbers 12:10.

46

She was turned white for seven days and put out of the camp until God restored her. It is fair to assume that they were dark skinned people for whom whiteness would be uncommon.

The scriptures also confirm that the Israelites were familiar with Egyptian theology. In Exodus 3:14 God instructs Moses to tell the Israelites that "I Am hath sent me." One of the names of the supreme deity of Egypt was Nuk Pu Nuk, which means "I Am that I Am."(10) Jesus also refers to himself as "I Am" when he was challenged by certain Jews (John 8:58), for which they tried to stone him to death. The use of "I Am" as an identifier of who Moses was representing would make perfect sense to an Egyptian, but is vaguely understood by modern Christians.

Similarly, the use of "Amen" in the Bible, and at the end of a Christian or Moslem prayer, has an Egyptian explanation. It is commonly defined as meaning "verily" or "so let it be." However, in Revelations 3:14 Jesus is identified as "the Amen, the faithful and true witness, the beginning of the creation of God." The capitalizing of Amen identifies it as a proper noun. Therefore, it is more than a common exclamation, it is an identifier of someone in particular. In ancient Egyptian mythology, "Amen" or "Amon" is the name of one of the facets of the supreme God. Historian Anthony Browder states that Amen is "the personification of the sun after setting, when it was hidden from view in the underworld."(11) Amen is also the creator of the other facets of God, which are called "Netcherw." It was sacred tradition that every Egyptian ruler should be a son of Amen.(12) This is why many of the Pharaohs prefixed their names with "Amen" (i.e. Amenemhet and Amenhotep). Jean-Francois Champollion reported the Egyptian's belief that

"Amon is the point of departure and the focal point of all divine essences." This is consistent with the theological status of Jesus Christ in Christianity.

According to Finch, an etymological examination of important names and phrases used in the Bible reveals more Egyptian connections, shown in Figure 1.(13)

The children of Israel also accepted Egyptian customs, starting with Joseph. Genesis 50:2 states that Joseph had his father's body embalmed. Embalming is a method of preserving a corpse that was started by the Egyptians and was not known among the Hebrews until Joseph had Jacob embalmed and placed in a coffin in Egypt. The practice was continued with the embalming of Joseph at his death. They also continued the practice of circumcision, an ancient Egyptian ritual.

In the 32nd chapter of Exodus the Israelites are called a "stiffnecked people" (verse 9) by God, because they made a golden calf to worship while Moses was away from them. The worship of the calf was an Egyptian practice and was a form of sun worship. In Egyptian cosmogony there are many different deities and representation of the sun. In one Egyptian myth, the sky is represented by a gigantic cow that gave birth to the sun. In this myth the sun is symbolized by a calf.(14) This form of worship was common to the Israelites according to Aaron from his statement to Moses: "Thou knowest the people, that they are set on mischief."

It is through Egypt that the children of Israel came into being. Some ancient traditions identify the Israelites as Egyptian or Ethiopian people. Tacitus, a first century Roman historian, reported that "many assert that the Jews are an Ethiopian race."(15) Strabo identifies the Jews as "a people originally from Egypt."

Figure 1: Egyptian and Hebrew words compared

EGYPTIAN TERMS	HEBREW TERMS
ATEM - The first god in the image of man.	ADAM - *Man;* the first man created by God.
QEN - To beat, strike down or murder.	QAYIN (Cain) - *Spear;* murdered his brother Abel.
NU-AKH - Flood waters that irrigate and fertilize the land.	NUACH (NOAH) - *Rest;* The builder of the ark.
AB-REM - Father of the people.	ABRAM - *Exalted father.*
IB-RA-IM - Desire or wisdom of Ra's fire.	ABRAHAM - *Father of a great multitude.*
YS-AKH - Place of burnt offering.	YSAC (ISAAC) - *Laughter;* The son Abraham offered as a sacrifies.
YS-RA-IR - Place of Ra's creation.	ISRAEL - *Having power with God.*
YAH-WAH - The growing moon.	YAHWEH - *Eternal one.*
JUHUDY - Name for the lunar diety Thoth.	JUHUDI (JUDEAN) - *Resident of Judea.*
SET - An evil infertile deity.	SATAN - *Adversary.*

NOTES

1) Murphy, Jefferson E. *History of African Civilization*, (Dell Publishing Co., Inc. New York, NY 1972) p. 31.
2) Bernal, Martin. *Black Athena Vol.2*, (Rutgers University Press, New Brunswick, NJ 1991) p. 321 and
   Van Sertima, Ivan and Runuko Rashidi, editors. *African Presence in Early Asia*, (Transaction Books, New Brunswick, NJ 1988) p. 190.
3) Bernal, *Black Athena Vol.2*, p. 357.
4) Van Sertima, *African Presence in Early Asia*, p. 191.
5) Bernal, *Black Athena Vol.2*, p. 359.
6) Ibid., p. 39.
7) Massey, Gerald. *Book of Beginnings Vol.2*, (Williams and Norgate, London, 1881) pp. 363-441.
8) Chapter 2, p. 27.
9) McCray, Rev. Walter Arthur. *The Black Presence in the Bible Vol.1*, (Black Light Fellowship, Chicago, IL 1990) p. 20.
10) Wheless, Joseph. *Is It God's Word?*, (Alfred A. Knopf, New York, NY 1926) p. 78.
11) Browder, Tony. *Nile Valley Contributions to Civilization*, (The Institute of Karmic Guidance, Washington D.C. 1992) p. 85.
12) Durant, Will. *The Story of Civilization, Part one: Our Oriental Heritage*, (Simon and Schuster, New York, 1954) p. 153.
13) Van Sertima, *African Presence in Early Asia*, pp. 193-196.
14) Budge, E.A. Wallis. *The Book of The Dead*, (University Books, Inc. Secaucus, NJ 1960) pp. 132-133.
15) Windsor, Rudolphf R. *The Valley of the Dry Bones*, (Windsor's Golden Series, Atlanta, GA 1986) pp. 60,62 and Massey, *Book of Beginnings Vol.2*, pp. 428-433.

CHAPTER 4

ISRAEL SCATTERED AMONG THE NATIONS

Based on the information provided in the first three chapters, several historical truths can be added to popular Christian history and several misconceptions and lies can be put to rest. It is true that the Egyptian people of the Bible were black; that the biblical Hebrews mixed with black Semitic (Syrians) and Hamitic (Egyptians and Canaanites), and that the children of Israel were an Egyptian people. These truths put to rest long believed misconceptions and lies that upset historical continuity and balance of the biblical story. It is not true that blackness was a curse imposed on black people because of Cain's killing Abel or Canaan being cursed by Noah.(1) It is not true that the biblical Israelites were white. To be black was natural for the Israelites. Furthermore, it is not true that Adam, Noah, Abraham, Isaac, Jacob, or any of the Old Testament figures were white.

Before the children of Israel entered Egypt around 1706 B.C., they were a mix of Hebrew-Egyptian people. When they departed from Egypt around 1491 B.C., they were an Egyptian people that became a distinct nation called "Israel." In the 22nd chapter of Numbers, King Balak of Moab recognized the Israelites as a people "from Egypt." They may be compared to the British colonists who left, or were put out of, England and became Americans, South Africans or Australians. Though they all came from England, they became distinct nations of people based upon similar social conditions, religious beliefs, political struggles and geographical boundaries.

If the Israelites would have remained a pure nation by not intermixing with other nations, there would be no question of the ethnicity of Jesus and his New Testament contemporaries. However, according to the Bible, the Israelites often offended God by taking wives of other nations. The offense was not an issue of ethnic purity or racial pride. The offense involved the worship of other gods that often occurred with intermixing.

The earliest Israelite laws instruct them to love the strangers among them and to treat them "as one born among" them.(2) Moses was married to a Midianite woman, yet this did not displease God. In the 25th chapter of Numbers, God is angered at the Israelites for worshipping the Moabite god Baal-Peor as a result of their intermixing with the Moabite women. For this offense, 24,000 men died from a plague. The plague was stopped by the actions of Aaron's grandson Phinehas (which means "the negro") when he killed an Israelite man and his Midianite companion. Because of his "zealous" action, Phinehas was blessed with a covenant of everlasting priesthood. (Numbers 25:6-13)

In the 31st chapter of Numbers, Israelite men were ordered to keep all of the Midianite girls who were virgins and to kill the women who were not virgins. These non-virgins were accused of causing the children of Israel to worship Baal-Peor and there was fear that they may continue to have this evil affect on the men of Israel. The number of virgin girls that the Israelite soldiers kept for themselves was 32,000. These girls probably became wives and concubines of the Israelites.

The following are scripture references detailing the Israelites intermixing with other nations and sometimes angering God by their idolatry:

Deuteronomy 23:7 - The Edomites are called a "brother" to Israel and the Israelites are instructed to not abhor the Edomites or the Egyptians and that their children may become members of Israel in their third generation.

Judges 3:5-8 - The Israelites mixed with the Canaanites, Hittites, Amorites, Perizzites, Hivites and Jebusites.

Judges 14:1-4 - Samson marries a Philistine woman.

Ruth 1:3,4 - Elimelech and Naomi's sons marry Moabite women; one of her Moabite daughter in-laws was Ruth.

Ruth 4:11-17 - Boaz and Ruth marry and give birth to Obed, the father of Jesse and grandfather of David. It is from this lineage that Jesus was born.

II Samuel 11:3 - Bathsheba is the wife of Uriah the Hittite. David arranged for Uriah to be killed in order to marry Bathsheba. This scripture shows that Hittites served in the Israelite army and that Hittites and Israelites intermixed.

I King 3:1 - Solomon marries the daughter of an Egyptian Pharaoh.

I King 11:1-4 - Solomon had 700 wives and 300 concubines. Among them were Moabites, Ammonites, Edomites, Zidonians and Hittites. God became angry with Solomon's idolatry.

I King 16:31 - King Ahab of Israel married Jezebel, a Zidonian. He angered God with his idolatry.

I Chronicles 2:3 - The sons of Judah were born of a Canaanite woman.

I Chronicles 2:17 - Jether, David's brother-in-law, was an Ishmaelite.

I Chronicles 2:35 -Sheshan, a leader of Judah, gives his daughter to Jarha, an Egyptian, to wed.

Ezra 9:1,2 - Ezra reports that the people of Israel, the priest, and the Levites have taken wives of the Canaanites, Hittites, Perizzites, Jebusites, Ammonites, Moabites, Egyptians and Amorites. He states that the rulers and princes were the most notorious offenders.

Ezra 10:2,18-44 - Ezra is informed that many of the Israelites have foreign wives and provides names of the fathers of those sons of Israel with strange wives.

Nehemiah 13:23-31 - Reports that the Jews were married to women of Ashdod, Ammon and Moab, and that their children could not speak the "Jew's language."

Esther 2-17 - Esther marries Ahasuerus, the king of Persia. As queen, she saved the lives of Jews when Haman plotted to kill them.

Ezekiel 23 - The "word of the lord" accused Samaria (Israelites) of intermixing with the Assyrians and Jerusalem (Judah) of mixing with the Chaldeans and Babylonians.

These scriptures identify specific people and nations that the Israelites/Jews mixed with. It is interesting to note that they only mixed with Hamitic and Semitic people. One possible exception is Esther's marriage to the king of Persia. The Persians are commonly considered Indo-European people. However, according to H.G. Wells, "There is a streak of very negroid blood traceable in south Persia and some parts of India."(3) The following statement from African historian Leo Hansberry further illuminates our understanding of Persian ethnicity:

The spread of the Aryan and the rise and spread of the Semitic and Mongolian peoples during the third and second millennium B.C. came into serious competition with the older black population, and in the clashes and racial intermixture which followed, distinctive black culture and ethnic traits were considerably dissipated. In some regions the original features were more definitely preserved; the Persian areas and its environs seems to have been one of these. In Persia the old Negroid element seems indeed to have been sufficiently powerful to maintain the overlordship of the land. For the Negritic strain is clearly evident in statuary depicting members of the royal family ruling in the second millennium B.C. Hundreds of years later, when Xerxes invaded Greece, the type was well represented in the Persian army.(4)

The acknowledgement of Ahasuerus (the Persian king that took Esther as his wife) as the ruler of 127 provinces from India to Ethiopia confirms his close relationship with lands occupied by black people south and west of Persia around 521 B.C.(Esther 1:1)

Around 940 B.C., Solomon was succeeded by his son Rehoboam as the king of Israel. Shortly after being made king, a civil conflict caused a revolution. The tribes of Judah and Benjamin (henceforth jointly called "Judah" or "Jews") were the only ones that remained loyal to Rehoboam. The other 10 tribes chose Jeroboam as the new king of Israel. The 12 tribes have never been reunited.

In 722 B.C. Israel was conquered by the Assyrians and ended as a national power. According to II Kings 17:6, the 10 tribes were carried away into Assyria, but some poorer Israelites were not taken. The Israelite cities left practically vacant after the expulsion were reoccupied by men from Babylon, Hamath and Sepharvaim. These people worshiped their own gods and were also trained in the worship of the God of Israel. Subsequently, the Israelites that were not taken and those foreigners trained in the worship of God came to be called "Samaritans."

The Samaritans were considered a mixed race by the Jews. It was bad enough that they were not pure Israelites and worshiped other gods. They also rejected Jerusalem as the center for true worship. David made Jerusalem the capital of Israel and Solomon built the temple there for the worship of

God. The Samaritans chose Mt. Gerizim, near the city of Shechem, as their center of worship. They believed Mt. Gerizim to be the site where Abraham was to sacrifice Isaac. The Jews and Samaritans remained at odds into New Testament times.

In 586 B.C. Judah was conquered by Nebuchadnezzer, king of Babylon, who carried all of the Jews away to Babylon, except the "poorer sort of the people of the land"(II King 24:14). Persia conquered Babylon in 539 B.C. Cyrus II was ruler of Persia and Media. He ended the Babylonian captivity of the Jews after 70 years and allowed 42,000 Jews to return to Jerusalem to rebuild the temple. The Jews grew stronger under Persian rule. It took 20 years for them to rebuild the temple, which was completed in 515 B.C.

Confirming the popular belief that the New Testament Jews were white must involve proving that they and/or the nations that they intermixed with were white people. The word "white" is used 46 times in the Old Testament and 23 of these uses refer to skin color. Of these 23 references to white skin, 22 are made regarding leprosy. The only reference not involving leprosy is in the 5th chapter of the Song of Solomon, wherein the lover (presumed to be Solomon) is called "white and ruddy." The allegorical nature of this scripture makes it difficult to conclude that Solomon had white skin. A similar use of "whiter" and "ruddy" is found in the 4th chapter of Lamentations about the Nazarites of Israel. Despite their being called "whiter than milk," this scripture also reports that their faces were "blacker than a coal." This reference to blackness seems to relate to a state of oppression.

The word "black" is used 15 times in the Old Testament and five of these uses refer to skin color. Of the five uses, three seem to imply blackness of the Israelites as a state of oppression, famine or depression (i.e. Job exclaimed, "My skin is black upon me and my bones are burned with heat").(5) The other two uses of "black" are made by the Shulamite woman in the Song of Solomon. She proclaimed, "I am black, but comely ....Look not upon me because I am black, because the sun hath looked upon me; my mother's children were angry with me; they made me the keeper of the vineyard." It is clear that her blackness is spoken of in connection with the oppression she experienced at the hands of her mother's children. The contemporary use of "black" is quite different from these Old Testament applications. Yet their skin becoming deep black implies melanin is present. A white person with a deep sunburn will be tan, red or brown, but certainly not black.

Of the nations that the Israelites mixed with in the Old Testament, none of them were European whites. The Old Testament, which concludes with the book of Malachi around 400 B.C., gives no examples of white nations or individuals intermixing with the Israelites. The 400 years between the Bible books of Malachi and Matthew are called the "Period of Silence" because the few existing writings from that period are not accepted as inspired or canonical. Professor of ancient history Morton Smith asserts that "cohabitation of Palestinian woman and Greek soldiers was frequent." He also reports that the Greek historian Hecataeus states, "Jewish intermixing with aliens was prevalent." This implies that the Jews intermixed with the Greeks without explicitly saying that the Palestinian women were Jews or that the aliens were Greeks.(6)

60

During these 400 years the Jews fell under Greek, Syrian and Roman domination. During the time of Nehemiah (444 B.C.) two different political movements existed among the Jews, which continued to impact Jewish history into New Testament times. The two movements involved one group of Jews that supported a separatist Jewish society and the other movement of Jews that wanted an assimilated Jewish society. The separatists advocated that Jews worship God (Yahweh) exclusively. They believed that the Gentiles ("ger" in Hebrew, which means "resident alien") could not become members of the Jewish people and they held very strict rules against intermixing. The assilmilationists created the legal status of "proselyte" for the ger. This status allowed aliens to accept the Jewish laws and enjoy the rights it conferred.(7)

Ezra and Nehemiah spoke strongly against intermixing and agreed that the Gentiles could not be declared ritualistically "purified" or "pure." According to the purity law, reported in Haggai 2:10-14, to mix with nations that worshiped other gods or to touch items used in the worship of other gods made a Jew impure, the same as touching something dead would make a Jew impure. However, Isaiah reported a new prophesy, which allowed aliens that followed Jewish laws to become pure as a natural Jew.(8)

This prophesy is one of the earliest doctrines that allowed non-Israelites/Jews to become people of the God of Abraham, Isaac and Jacob. Before this belief, God (Yahweh) exclusively was the national god of the Israelites. This doctrine of assimilation prepared the way for Christianity by allowing non-Jews to receive the blessings and promises of God by accepting the Jewish laws. In New Testament teachings, these blessings are conferred by accepting Jesus as one's personal savior instead of accepting Jewish laws. This change from accepting Judaism to accepting Jesus was quite controversial and will be discussed in the 7th chapter.

It is likely that there were rare instances of intermixing between Jews and European whites, but not without complications. In addition to Jewish laws restricting intermixing, the Greeks also had laws against intermarriage. Language and cultural differences also served as barriers to intermixing. The separatist mindset continued into New Testament times. The Pharisees, which literally means "to separate," were a separatist party that originated from the earlier separatist movement. They wanted to make Jewish laity just as pure as the priest.(9) Greek, Syrian and Roman domination of Palestine will be examined in the next chapter, in connection with the political impact they had on New Testament times and the life of Jesus.

NOTES

1) One theory of blackness as a curse asserts that the "mark" God placed on Cain, in Genesis 4:15, was blackness. Another more popular theory asserts that blackness and slavery were imposed on black people when Noah cursed Canaan in Genesis 9:24-29.

2) *The African Heritage Study Bible*, King James Version (The James C. Winston Publishing Company, Nashville, TN 1993) Leviticus 19:33-34 and Exodus 22:21.

3) Wells, H.G. *The Outline of History*, (The MacMillan Company, New York, NY 1921) p. 109.

4) Harris, Joseph E., Editor. *Africa & Africans As Seen by Classical Writers*, (Howard University Press, Washington D.C., 1977) p. 52.

5) *The African Heritage Study Bible*, Job 30:30.

6) Smith, Morton. *Palestinian Parties and Politics That Shaped the Old Testament*, (SCM Press Ltd., London, 1987) p. 65.

7) Ibid., p. 139.

8) Gottwald, Norman K. *All The Kingdoms of the Earth*, (Harper & Row Publishers, New York, 1964) p. 385 and *The African Heritage Study Bible*, Isaiah 56:1-8.

9) Pentecost, J. Dwight. *The Words and Works of Jesus Christ*, (Academie Books of Zondervan Publishing House, Grand Rapids, MI, 1981) pp. 542-553.

CHAPTER 5

GREEK AND ROMAN RULE OVER PALESTINE

The Old Testament ends with the Jews under Persian rule. In 333 B.C. Palestine fell under Greek rule through the leadership of Alexander "the Great," who was met in Jerusalem by a peaceful procession of Jews led by the High Priest to surrender to Greek authority.(1) He conquered Egypt in 332 B.C. and founded the city of Alexandria. At the invitation of Alexander, a large colony of Jews migrated to Alexandria and later grew to be the largest home of Jews outside of Palestine. Aside from Jews, Alexandrian citizenry also included many Greeks, Persians, Syrians and Egyptians.(2)

Despite Greek and Roman rule, the Palestinian region maintained its population of Semitic and Hamitic people. According to Strabo, at the end of the first century the territory around Jerusalem was "inhabited in general, as is each place in particular, by mixed stocks of people from Egyptian [by which he means Jewish] and Arabian and Phoenician tribes; such, moreover, are those who occupy Galilee and Jericho and Philadelphia and Samaria."(3)

In 323 B.C. Alexander died and the lands conquered by him were divided among his generals. General Ptolemy I Sotar gained control of Egypt and Palestine. In addition to having a museum built in Alexandria, he is well known for using Egyptian ideologies to produce a national deity called "Serapis." Ptolemy I declared that he was given a revelation in a dream, which revealed to him the image of Serapis. A statue was immediately constructed and the resulting image is remarkably similar to the popular white portrayal of Jesus. According to author Walter Williams, "this icon/image was a predecessor of the Jesus Christ Image."(4) The worship of Serapis gained much support in Greece, Asia Minor, Sicily and Rome. It was not well received by the Egyptians and resisted by the monotheistic Jews and Persians.

Ptolemy II Philadelphus succeeded his father in 285 B.C. and was considered a friend to the Jews. Many more Jews moved to Egypt during his rule. Two of his greatest accomplishments were the founding of the Library of Alexandria and having the Hebrew scriptures translated into Greek, the common language of the time. According to tradition, it took 72 Jewish scholars 72 days to produce this Greek version of the Pentatuch, the Hebrew version of the first five books. The Letter of Aristeas, written by a courier of Ptolemy II to his brother, reports that six leading scholars were chosen from each tribe. He also describes the conflicts that existed between the Hellenic Jews of Alexandria and the Hebraic Jews of Palestine. It took more than 200 years to translate all of the Hebrew writings. This Greek version of the Old Testament is called the Septuagint, which means "seventy." Bible historian Dr. Neil R. Lightfoot says, "It is believed that the version was completed at Alexandria, but probably by Alexandrian rather than Palestinian Jews."(5) Scriptures from the Septuagint were often quoted by Jesus and other New Testament figures.

In 204 B.C. the Seleucidae rulers of Syria gained control of Palestine. Seleucus I Nicator, another one of Alexander's generals, became the first ruler of this dynasty in 323 B.C. The fifth successor of the dynasty, Antiochus IV Epiphanes, seized control of Palestine from the Ptolemies. At this time the land was divided into five provinces. These provinces were Judea,

Samaria, Galilee, Trachonitis and Perea. Antiochus IV greatly persecuted the Jews. His contemporaries considered him to be "a madman" and "unqualifiedly demented." He had 40,000 Jews put to death, sold many others into slavery and profaned the Temple in Jerusalem by offering a pig on its alter. Further persecution included restricting synagogue services, the re-dedication of the Jerusalem Temple to the god Zeus, declaring circumcision a capital offense and declaring observance of the Sabbath an act of treason.(6)

The oppressed Jews responded with an insurrection led by a priest named Mattathias. He gained fame by killing two of Antiochus' commissioners and an apostate Jew who was worshipping at an idol alter. Despite being up in age, he led an army into the mountains of Judea and conducted guerilla warfare against the forces of Antiochus IV. Mattathias fought until his death and was succeeded by Judas, one of his five sons. Judas lead his inferior Jewish forces to victory in three decisive battles against the forces of Antiochus IV. The Seleucidae ruler died of disease while making new plans to increase persecution of the Jews.

Judas was given the name Maccabaeus, meaning "the hammerer," because of his successful leadership in war. Judas Maccabaeus became the Priest-King of Judea in 163 B.C. and the Maccabees' Hasmonian dynasty (named after Hasmon, an ancestor of Mattathias) maintained independent rule in Palestine until a civil war erupted in Judea. The conflict resulted from disputed claims between Aristobulus II and John Hyrcanus II, both decendants of Mattathias. The claims were submitted for arbitration to Pompey, a Roman general. Pompey favored the claim of Hyrcanus II. Aristobulus II continued to dispute the decision and was defeated in battle by Pompey, who took control of Jerusalem and appointed Hyrcanus II ethnarch (provincial governor) of Palestine in 63 B.C.

A Jewish relationship with the Romans was first established through a treaty of friendship initiated by Simon, the third son of Mattathias and the fourth Priest-King of the Hasmonian dynasty. This treaty was renewed by Hyrcanus II. The title of "ethnarch" emphasizes the fact that Judea then became one of many provinces of the Roman empire.(7) While under Roman rule, the Jews were given full religious rights and political liberty, but they were made to pay a yearly tribute.

Around 47 B.C. Roman Emperor Julius Caesar appointed Hyrcanus II as the King of Judea and appointed Antipater, a wealthy Idumean (Edomite) officer, its procurator. He also appointed Herod, Antipater's son, as governor of Galilee. Herod grew in power and later married Mariamne, the granddaughter of Hyrcanus II. Political conflicts in Rome led to the assassination of Julius Caesar. The conspirators in the assassination were forced into exile by Mark Antony, who gained almost complete control of the Roman empire. Around 40 B.C. Antony appointed Herod as the King of Judea. It was this Herod that the New Testament identifies as having Jewish babies put to death out of fear that the long awaited Messiah was born.

During Greek and Roman rule many Jews accepted some elements of the Hellenistic culture (Greek style of dress, language, names and ideas). Hellenistic Jews were commonly found in Alexandria and the Galilee region of Palestine, but not in Judea. The Judeans maintained a strong commitment to Jewish ideas and customs. After years of subjugation to other nations, the Hebrew language was no longer common to the Jews. After the Babylonian exile, most of them spoke Aramaic. It was the language of the Syrians (or Aramites) that was spoken by the Babylonians after 1000 B.C. and was also the official language of the Persian empire after 500 B.C. In the first century A.D. some Jews spoke Koine, a tongue that resulted from the fusion of classical Greek and the commercial vernacular of Near Eastern people. The entire New Testament was written in Koine.(8)

There were five principle sects or political parties among the New Testament Jews. These five parties were the Pharisees, Sadducees, Essenes, Zealots and Herodians. The Pharisees (which means "to separate") strongly resisted foreign influence and observed the Jewish laws with legalistic fervor. They also believed in an afterlife and resurrection.

The Sadducees were composed of Jewish aristocrats and held many important positions on the Sanhedrin, which served as the supreme judicial council of the Jews. It was the Sanhedrin that found Jesus guilty of blasphemy, which led to his crucifixion. The Sadducees were ultraconservative and placed much emphasis on politics and none on religion.

The Essenes were a sect that lived an isolated communal life west of the Dead Sea. Their lives consisted of reading the scriptures, having worship services and sometimes engaging in a baptism ritual. The Essenes are not mentioned in the Bible but, they were a major sect during New Testament times.

The Zealots were the revolutionary Jews who wanted to gain their independence through war with Rome. Judas Iscariot, the betrayer of Jesus, was a member of this group.

The Herodians were supporters of the government of Herod. They believed that this foreign (Idumean) rule provided the best hope for protection of their lives and property.(9)

Popular among the Jews was the anticipation of the "Expected One" who would come to deliver them from their foreign rulers. They anticipated that this king would lead them in physical battle against the foreign rulers, restore the Temple and reunify the 12 tribes of Israel. The book of Daniel foretold of the "Ancient of Days" that would give "glory and kingship" to "one like a Son of Man." It was expected that he would be a "Son (descendant) of David." Millions of people believe that Jesus was, and is, this "Expected One" and has been given the title "Messiah" or "Christ," both of which mean "anointed one."

NOTES

1) Pentecost, J. Dwight. *The Words and Works of Jesus Christ*, (Academie Books of Zondervan Publishing House, Grand Rapids, MI 1981) p. 530.
2) Radin, Max. *The Jews Among the Greeks and Romans*, (Jewish Publication Society of America, Philidelphia, PA 1915) p. 92.
3) Smith, Morton. *Palestinian Parties and Politics that Shaped the Old Testament*, (SCM Press LTD, London 1987) p. 65.
4) Williams, Walter. *The Historical Origin of Christianity*, (Maathian Press, Inc. Chicago, IL 1992) p. iii and Kamil, Jill. *Coptic Egypt*, (The American University in Cairo Press, Cairo, Egypt 1987) p. 20.
5) Lightfoot, Neil R. *How We Got the Bible*, (Baker Book House, Grand Rapids, MI 1963) p. 73 and Harris, Stephen L. *Understanding the Bible*, (Mayfield Publishing Company, Palo Alto, CA 1980) pp. 191-192.
6) Radin, *The Jews Among the Greeks and Romans*, pp. 136,143.
7) Harris, *Understanding the Bible*, p. 213.
8) Ibid., p. 7.
9) Pentecost, *The Words and Works of Jesus Christ*, p. 542.

CHAPTER 6

THE BIBLICAL AND HISTORICAL JESUS

The Apostles' Creed states that Jesus is the Son of God, "who was born of Mary the Virgin, was crucified under Pontius Pilate, on the third day rose from the dead, ascended into Heaven, sittith on the right hand of the Father, from which he cometh to judge the living and the dead."(1)

It is believed that Jesus was born around 4 B.C., probably in March or April, and was put to death April 4, 33 A.D.(2) Most people assume the story of Jesus is well documented biblically and historically. This may or may not be true, based on what one is willing to believe.

From a biblical perspective, many Bible scholars have doubts about who the authors of the New Testament books were and when the books (or letters) were written. Most scholars agree that Mark was the first of the Gospels written, and was followed by Matthew, Luke and John. The later writers most likely used the book of Mark and added the stories of Jesus' birth. Since the beginning of Christianity, there have been controversies about which books should be canonized (accepted as truly God-inspired Christian literature) and which ones to declare heresy. In fact, the books of Peter, James, Jude, Hebrews and Revelation were all heavily disputed by some early Christians.(3)

Some of the Apostles of Jesus (the 12 men trained and commissioned by Jesus personally) doubted the authenticity of Paul's conversion and his authority as an apostle, an issue still debated. There are many Christian ministers today who reject his authority. These and other matters produce some difficulty in developing historical certainty regarding the life of Jesus, and cause complications in developing religious doctrines for Christians to live by.

From a historical perspective, there is no widely accepted evidence from the time Jesus lived to verify that he ever existed. The Bible and non-canonical documents that support the existence of Jesus are often dismissed by critics as subjective Christian propaganda and myth. They were all written years after the time Jesus is believed to have lived. The lack of evidence current to the time of Jesus does not mean that he never existed. It may mean that the Christian writers developed a better understanding of the ministry and personal history of Jesus after the time of his death and resurrection.

There also exists non-Christian references to the existence of Jesus. The 1st century Roman historian Tacitus reported that a man called "Christus" was executed under Tiberius and Pontius Pilate. The report about Jesus by Josephus is given in his *The Antiquities of the Jews*, though not preserved in its original form.(4)

Gerald Massey rejects these sources as "forgeries" and argues that the lack of "contemporary testimony or recognition" is due to the biblical Jesus being a mythical figure based on a 1st century B.C. man named Jehoshua ben Pandira, as recorded in the Talmud. "Jehoshua" (or "Yehoshua") is the original Aramaic for the more popular Greek version of the name "Jesus." The Talmud reports that Jehoshua was trained in Egypt, performed many miracles and was put to death as a sorcerer.(5)

It took many years for the biblical image of Jesus to crystalize. The nature of Christ was still being disputed by

74

church leaders well into the 5th century B.C. and the development of the many different Christian denominations resulted from varying interpretations.

The acknowledgement of Jesus as "Christ" is the most important element of the Christian religion. The title "Christ" is derived from the Greek term "Christos," which means "the anointed." It is equivalent to the Hebrew "mashiackh," from which the word "messiah" is derived. There is also a belief that the term "Christ" has some affinity to the Egyptian term "karast," which refers to the mummification process of embalming a corpse, perfuming it and standing it upright. The common Hebrew concept of anointing involved the belief that a person anointed with certain oils gained superior or supernatural powers.

According to J.A. Rogers, "Christ" comes from the Indian term "Krishna" or "Chrishna," meaning "The Black One." However, the Society for Krisna Consciousness teaches that "Krisna" means "all attractive."(6)

The pre-Christian era Jewish anticipation of an "Expected One" was expressed in the post-Christian era as the "Christ." The recognition of Jesus as Christ did not come easy and the establishing of Christianity as a religion independent of Judaism took many years.

It is difficult to establish biblical and historical consensus about the life of Jesus. The issue of how early Christians depicted him physically is just as complicated and probably more controversial.

Since the 2nd century, there have been physical depictions made of Jesus. The Bible gives no description of him. In the book of Isaiah (Chapter 53, Verse 2) a prophesy is given that is accepted as being about Jesus, which says "he has no form or comeliness; and when we shall see him, there is no beauty that we should desire him." In Revelations 1:15 and Daniel 7:9 he is described, somewhat metaphorically, as having hair like "wool" and feet like burned brass.

In the 4th century one depiction of Jesus became quite popular. This image was based on the *Letter of Lentulus*, supposedly written by a Roman official named Lentulus during the time Jesus lived. The letter has no credibility and was probably a medieval Latin forgery. Lentulus was Pontius Pilate's superior and was believed to have written a report to Tiberius Caesar, including a warrant for the arrest of Jesus that provided this physical description:

At this time there appeared and is still living a man, if indeed he can be called a man at all, of great powers named the Christ, who is called Jesus. The people term him the prophet of truth; his disciples call him Son of God, who wakens the dead and heals the sick, a man of erect stature, of medium height, fifteen and a half fist high, of temperate and estimable appearance, with a manner inspiring of respect, nut-brown hair which is smooth to the ears and from the ears downward shaped in gentle locks and flowing down over the shoulders in ample curls, parted in the middle after the manner of the Nazarenes, with an even and clear brow, a face without spot or wrinkles, and of healthy color. Nose and mouth are flawless; he wears a luxuriant beard of the color of his hair. He has a simple and mature gaze, large, blue-grey eyes that are uncommonly varied in expressiveness, fearsome when he scolds and gentle and affectionate when he admonishes. He is gravely cheerful, weeps often, but has never been seen to laugh. In figure he is upright and straight. His hands and arms are well shaped. In conversation he is grave, mild and modest, so that the word of the prophet concerning the 'fairest of the sons of men' (Psalms 45:2) can be applied to him."(7)

This letter lacks credibility because of its blatant flattery of Jesus, uncommon for a Roman official. Its identification of Jesus as the "Christ," "Son of God" and "Prophet of truth" were all ascribed to him long after his death. The use of a scriptural reference further proves that it was written by a Christian supporter of Jesus and not a Roman official who wanted to arrest him.

In 705 A.D., during the second rule of the Roman Emperor Justinian II, a gold coin was minted that had Justinian and Tiberius on one side and Jesus on the other. The image of Jesus on this coin was of a man with an afro, facial hair of crisp curls, thick lips and a full nose. This African image replaced a more European image that appeared on an earlier coin.(8)

Paintings of Jesus from the 2nd and 3rd centuries A.D. are found in the Catacomb of Dormitilla. One painting shows a profile of a man with a thin nose, thin lips, very dark skin and black hair. Another painting, called "The Good Shepherd," shows a very dark skinned young man with an afro-like hair style.(9)

There are no known portrayals of Jesus from the 1st century A.D. and very few assigned to the 2nd century. Jesus did not become a hero to European people until more than 300 years after his death. They had no reason to honor him with portraits and statues. The Christians were basically considered enemies of Rome until the 4th century A.D. when, under the rule of Constantine, the Edict of Milan ended persecution of the Christians. After the reign of Constantine, Christianity was made the official religion of the Roman empire.

Unlike today, they had no cameras, video tapes or computers to record and maintain an accurate image of Jesus or his contemporaries. Under Roman persecution, the destruction of Christian literature and symbols often occured. This may account for the lack of images of Jesus from Christian communities of the first 300 years of the religion. It is unwise to expect a former oppressor to depict the national heros of its former enemy accurately 300 years after their deaths. The Romans could not defeat the Christians so they absorbed them into Roman culture in the 4th century. This assimilation produced a synthesized version of the religion and synthesized images to represent the religion. However, there were a few images produced in Rome that depict Jesus as a black man, such as the 7th century gold coin shown on page 81.

Despite the lack of early images, the portrayals of Jesus and Mary, popularly known as the "Black Madonna and Child," remains as positive proof that they were perceived as black people. In 1125 A.D. Rupert the Benedictine stated that paintings of Mary, common to his time, show her as "dark" and "black."(10) Today, there may be as many as 600 Black Madonnas, mostly in Europe.

In the 16th century A.D. there were 190 known Black Madonnas in France and today there may be as many as 300 there. According to William Mosley, author of *What Color Was*

Jesus? "hundreds of thousands make the annual pilgrimage to the Shrine of the Black Madonna at Alt-Otting in West Germany." He also states that "many believe that through contact with these images one can be healed of sickness and diseases, and there have been many published reports to that effect. *The Black Virgin of Kazan*, also called 'the miracle Ikon of Holy Russia,' is noted for the alleged miracles it has performed."(11)

The fact that Jesus was a 1st century Jew supports the belief that he was a black man. In his family lineage are found Hamite women (Tamar, Rahab and Bathsheba). He was of the tribe of Judah, considered a rabbi (teacher) by his contemporaries and allowed to teach in the synagogue. This respect and authority would not have been given to him if he were not perceived as a pure Jew.

There is no sin in seeing Jesus as a black man. Many people say that it does not matter what color he was, yet they refuse to replace their "white Jesus" image with a black one. Some people choose to use no image, but this will not erase the white image embedded in their minds.

The biblical Jesus was a black man. As a carpenter he was physically strong. He lived part of his life with no father. He came from Nazareth, a town in the Galilee region of Palestine where the people had the reputation of being of "passionate and lawless character."(12) He was considered a threat by the established political and religious leaders. He was a revolutionary who chose to change the world with a sword of truth. He was tried as a criminal and put to death.

Many black youth would benefit from knowing this perspective of Jesus. Like Jesus, many of today's black youth

79

work as laborers; they are fatherless; they live in communities where the people have the reputation of being lawless; they are considered a threat to society; and they are tried as criminals and put in prison to die. It may not matter to some people what color Jesus was, but it may make the difference to those who have rejected the Gospel as "the white man's religion."

Figure 1

A 7th century gold Roman coin showing an image of Jesus. This black image replaced a earlier white depiction of Jesus. (Picture provided courtesy of Dr. Charles Finch,III.)

NOTES

1) Latourette, Kenneth Scott. *A History of Christianity Vol.I*, (Harper & Row, Publishers, New York, NY 1975) p. 135.

2) Pentecost, J. Dwight. *The Words and Works of Jesus Christ*, (Academie Books of Zondervan Publishing House, Grand Rapids, MI 1981) pp. 56-57,572.

3) Harris, Stephen L. *Understanding The Bible*, (Mayfield Publishing Company, Palo Alto, CA 1980) p. 19.

4) Koester, Helmut. *History and Literature of Early Christianity Vol.2*, (Walter De Gruyter, New York, NY 1987) p. 14 and Harris, *Understanding the Bible*, p. 220.

5) Massey, Gerald. *The Historical Jesus and The Mythical Christ*, (A&B Books Publishing, Brooklyn, NY 1992) pp. 188-191.

6) Rogers, J.A. *Sex and Race Vol.I*, (Helga M. Rodgers, St. Petersburg, FL 1967) p. 265 and Prabhupada, A.C. Bhaktivedanta Swami. *Srimad Bhagavatam sixth Canto Part-One*, (The Bhaktivedante Book Trust, Los Angeles, CA 1979) p. 234.

7) Benz, Ernst. *The Eastern Orthodox Church*, (Anchor Books of Doubleday & Company, Inc., Garden City, NY 1963)pp.12-13.

8) Watts, Daud Malik. *The Black Presence in the Land of the Bible*, (Afro Vision, Inc., Washington D.C. 1990) pp. 22-23.

9) Comay, Joan and Ronald Brownrigg. *Who's Who in the Bible*, (Bonanza Books, New York, NY 1980) pp. 155,179.

10) Johnson, John L. *The Black Biblical Heritage*, (Winston-Derek Publishers, Inc., Nashville, TN 1993) p. 203.

11) Watts, *The Black Presence in the Land of the Bible*, p. 18 and Mosley, Williams. *What Color Was Jesus*, (African American Images, Chicago, IL 1987) p. 20.

12) Pentecost, *The Words and Works of Jesus Christ*, p. 521.

CHAPTER 7

JESUS' DISCIPLES AND APOSTLES

The biblical Jews of Palestine were a people subject to factionalism, split into several different religious and political cliques. The most influential sects were the Pharisees, Sadducees, Essenes, Zealots and Herodians (described in Chapter 5). The movement headed by Jesus was not considered a major sect during his life.

The story of Jesus is presented as the central theme of the New Testament. The Bible presents a report on the life of Jesus, which gives the reader the impression that his ministry "spread like wild fire" immediately following the resurrection. However, it took almost 500 years for the impact of the ministry of Jesus to spread slowly and grow as a world power. Responsible for initiating this growth process were the disciples and Apostles of Jesus. The word "disciple" represents the Greek word "matheteuo," which means to become a pupil or learner. According to J. Dwight Pentecost, author of *The Words and Works of Jesus Christ*, being a disciple "does not suggest that one accepts the word of a teacher, only that he will listen." The word "apostle" comes from the Greek word "apostolos," which means messenger or "he that is sent." The Apostles held the special status of being those personally sent by Jesus and endowed with the authority given to him by God.

It is fair to conclude that the Apostles and disciples were black Jews. There is no reason to assume that they were white, as they are popularly portrayed. There may have been a few white Gentiles who became proselytes, and lived according to Jewish laws. There were some instances of intermixing by a few

Hellenized Jews (Eunice is one example, Acts 16:1). However, they would be treated like the Samaritans, with scorn if they worshiped any other Gods.

The Romans looked upon intermixing with displeasure and had laws against intermarriage, as did the Greeks. Peter speaks of these laws in Acts 10:28, where he states, "It is an unlawful thing for a man that is a Jew to keep company, or come unto one of another nation." It is important to understand that laws and customs restricting intermixing among the Jews, Greeks and Romans were not based on race. In the 4th century B.C., Constantine is quoted as saying, "Every animal is prompted by nature to seek a mate among the animal of his own species and as the human species is divided into various tribes by the distinction of language, religion, and manners, a just regard to the purity of descent preserves the harmony of public and private life."(1) This statement says nothing about race and the present type of racism didn't exist in the Roman Empire. Septimus Severus, an African, was the Emperor of Rome from 193 to 211 A.D. and there were many different races of people among the Roman citizenry. The Apostle Paul was a Roman citizen, though he was a Jew.(2)

A Gentile could become a Jew by accepting Jewish laws, which included the worship of God (Yahweh) only, and being circumcised. This was a price that most Gentiles would not pay. The difficulty in properly converting Gentiles was expressed by Jesus in the New Testament (Matthew 23:15), where he states, "Woe unto the scribes and Pharisees, hypocrites! For ye compass sea and land to make one proselyte (converted Gentile), and when he is made, ye make him twofold more the child of hell then yourselves." Undoubtedly, the scribes and

84

Pharisees did not properly convert some Gentiles in Jesus' lifetime.

Purity was a major issue for the Jews of Palestine because they were the last stronghold of the worship of God (Yahweh) exclusively and the hope for the re-establishment of Israel. The teachings of Jesus seemed to represent the aspirations of many staunch Jews. He attracted many students with his teachings.

The "disciples of Jesus," when stated in the New Testament Gospels, generally refers to the 12 Apostles. These 12 men were symbolic of the 12 tribes of Israel. Most of them were unlearned men of lower status. Jesus had many more disciples, probably thousands. John, one of the 12, reported on a man casting out demons in the name of Jesus, though the man did not "follow" with them. Many disciples stopped following Jesus because of his unorthodox teachings (John 6:60-66) and "all the disciples forsook him" when he was arrested and taken to be crucified (Matthew 26:56). It was customary for one Jewish prisoner to be released during the Passover season. Jesus had become so unpopular that the Jews demanded that he be crucified for blasphemy, and chose to release a murdering thief named Barabbas.

The events recorded in the Bible following the trial of Jesus provide the foundation for Christian theology. These events begin with the death of Jesus on the cross. On the third day he was resurrected from the dead. He appeared before the disciples and many other people several times over a 40-day period. He commissioned the disciples to "go and make disciples of all nations" (Matthew 28:19). He ascended into the sky from the Mount of Olives. Two angels appeared, stating that Jesus would return "in like manner as ye have seen him go into heaven"(Acts 1:11).

On the day of Pentecost (an annual feast) in Jerusalem, 120 followers of Jesus received the "Holy Spirit" (also called the Comforter) while praying in the "Upper Room." The spirit gave them the ability to speak the languages of other people. There were Jews from many nations in Jerusalem for the feast and "they were all amazed...saying 'Behold, are not all these which speak Galilaeans?'(Acts 2:5-7)." This scripture provides the nationalities of these Jews as Parthians, Medes, Elamites, Mesopotamians, Judaens, Cappadocians, Phrygians, Pamphylians, Egyptians, Libyans, Cretes and Arabians. These were all Near East Asian and African people. It also states that there were "strangers of Rome" present who were Jews and proselytes. Rome is the only European nation mentioned. Identifying them as "strangers" is a clear indication that they were not considered familiar Jews like the Near East Asian and African Jews.

The spread of Christianity during the 1st century A.D. was led by the Apostles. Eleven of them were personally chosen by Jesus. Their names were Simon Peter, Andrew, James (son of Zebedee), John, Philip, Bartholomew, Thomas, Matthew, James (son of Alphaeus), Thaddaeus (or Judas, son of James) and Simon the Zealot. The apostles later chose Matthias, to replace Judas Iscariot, who hung himself after betraying Jesus.

Jesus told these men, "Ye shall be witnesses unto me both in Jerusalem, and in all Judaea, and in Samaria and unto the uttermost parts of the earth (Acts 1:8)." The Bible reports that the followers of Jesus were first called "Christians" (a word used only once in the Bible, in Acts 11:26) in Antioch, Syria.

From a theological perspective, they were empowered with

the Holy Spirit to spread the Gospel (means good news) of Jesus. This Gospel of Jesus involved teaching that Jesus was the "Expected One" and "Messiah" of the Jews and that he established a spiritual Kingdom of Israel where the believers would enjoy eternal life. They taught that Jesus, through his death and resurrection, became the symbol of true life and victory over death and sin. They taught that all people would be judged by Jesus on "Judgement Day" and through belief in Jesus as their Savior they would avoid the punishment of hell's fires.

The Old Testament laws, given through Moses, were therefore replaced by a New Testament gospel, given through Jesus. The word "testament" means covenant. The old covenant involved the Israelites observance of laws given to Moses by God. By strict observance of these laws, the Israelites enjoyed the blessings and favor of being the "Chosen People" of God (Yahweh). The new covenant involved a personal commitment to God through belief in Jesus. Through the belief and acceptance of the teachings of Jesus, an individual received the Holy Spirit and special spiritual gifts.

Before the new covenant, God (Yahweh) was the primary god of Israel and they were his people. Likewise, Amen was the primary god of Upper (southern) Egypt, and Baal was the primary god of the Canaanites. After the new covenant, God was presented as the only true God and Creator of the world, rather then a mere national deity. Jesus is presented as a sort of personal deity, through which an individual became a "child of God." Therefore, an individuals relationship with God became dependent upon their personal relationship with Jesus, rather than their being a Jew or by only observing Jewish laws.

87

It was this belief system that the Apostles began to spread around 35 A.D. The 1st century Christians were often forced to meet in secrecy because their teachings greatly clashed with orthodox Jewish beliefs. The Jewish authorities sought to stop the spread of Christianity by force. They authorized a Hellenized Jew, named Saul, to persecute and imprison Christians. However, Saul later became the most influential Christian figure of the 1st century, known as the Apostle Paul.

Paul claimed that he personally met Jesus during a miraculous encounter on the road to Damascus, and was commissioned by Jesus to be "a chosen vessel" to bear the name of Jesus "before the Gentiles, and kings, and the children of Israel."(Acts 9:15) Based on this encounter, Paul is counted as an apostle, the same as the original 12. Paul's first meeting with an original apostle was held three years after his conversion when he spent 15 days in Jerusalem with Peter. The teachings of Paul produced a conflict with Jerusalem church leaders and he was pressured to leave Jerusalem.

Though the original Apostles were personally trained and commissioned by Jesus to spread his teachings, Paul is credited with having done more to spread the religion then they. The New Testament of the Bible is composed of 27 books by seven writers, and 13 of them are believed to have been written by Paul.

The Bible confirms that Paul had the physical appearance of an Egyptian. In Acts 21:38 A Roman officer mistook Paul to be a certain Egyptian. Paul had to specify that he was a Jew. It appears that the Egyptians and Jews had physical characteristics indistinguishable to some Romans.

Paul's ministry emphasized the converting of Gentiles. In teaching these Christian proselytes, Paul was of the opinion that they did not have to observe all of the Jewish laws. Paul taught that Gentiles did not have to be circumcised and that they may eat food offered to idol gods. He de-emphasized observance of the Jewish Laws.

Peter was the main leader of the apostles and James (also called James the Just), the brother of Jesus, became the head of the Christian community in Jerusalem. They represented a segment of 1st century Christians called "Judaizers." Their belief in Jesus as the Messiah did not preclude their obedience of the Jewish laws. Non-Jewish converts to Christianity were expected to observe the Jewish Laws, just as earlier proselytes.(3) This matter was the earliest major controversy to effect the new religion. During Paul's last visit to Jerusalem in 58 A.D., the Judaizers tried to kill him for teaching against the Jewish laws. Peter later accepted similar belief to Paul's.

The remainder of this chapter provides brief biographies of the most notable apostles, New Testament authors, deacons, disciples and believers who spread the Christian religion during the 1st century. As Jews, they are all presumed to be black people.

Apostles

Andrew: He was a native of the fishing town Bethsaida, the brother of Simon Peter, and a former disciple of John the Baptist. He was one of the first disciples of Jesus. According to Eusebius, Andrew was sent to minister in Scythia.(4) *The Acts of St. Andrew*, an apocryphal writing, reports on his ministry and crucifixion in 60 A.D. at Patrae, a harbor city in Achaia.

Bartholomew: It is believed that he was also called Nathaniel in the Bible. According to tradition, he was killed in Armenia by having the skin ripped from his body.

James, son of Alphaeus: He was present in the Upper Room on the day of Pentecost. It is possible that he was the brother of Matthew. Nothing is known about his ministry after the crucifixion.

James, son of Zebedee: He was called "James the Great." He was the brother of John. James, Peter and John formed an inner circle of three men who were closest to Jesus. He was the first apostle to be put to death and the only apostle who's martyrdom is reported in the Bible. He was beheaded by Herod Agrippa.

John: He was the brother of James the Great and member of Jesus' inner circle, along with James and Peter. He and his brother were called "the sons of thunder" by Jesus. He reportedly led a ministry in Ephesus and was exiled to the Island of Patmos by Emperor Domitian. He is believed to be the author of the book of John, I John, II John, III John and Revelations. Eusibius reports that he was put to death in Ephesus.

Matthew: He was a tax collector, recruited by Jesus from Capernaum. He is believed to be the author of the first gospel, based on the report of Papias, bishop of Hieropolis (60-130 A.D.), who stated that Matthew made a collection of the sayings of Jesus in Hebrew. One tradition reports of his martyrdom in Ethiopia.(5)

Matthias: He was a loyal disciple of Jesus before the crucifixion. He is mentioned only once in the Bible as being chosen to replace Judas Iscariot, who hung himself after betraying Jesus. There is a tradition that places him in Ethiopia.

Paul: Formerly called Saul of Tarsus. He was a Hellenized Jew, and well trained in the Hebrew laws. He was a Roman citizen, a status not common to most Jews. He was the only apostle who did not know Jesus personally. He participated in the persecution of Christians and was responsible for the imprisonment and murder of many. He was converted to Christianity around 35 A.D. and ministered to the Gentile nations for about 30 years. He was the only apostle reported in the Bible to focus his ministry on the European nations. This caused him to be hated among Christian and non-Christian Jews. Thirteen of the biblical Epistles identify him as the author, and some scholars believe him to be the author of the book of Hebrews. Sometime between 62 and 67 A.D., Paul was

91

kept under house arrest in Rome, where he was allowed to receive guests and write many letters. Popular tradition says he was put to death in 67 A.D. by the Emperor Nero by being beheaded in or near Rome.

Philip: He was probably a disciple of John the Baptist and was recruited by Jesus on the bank of the River Jordan. One tradition says he died naturally at Hierapolis, while another tradition says he was crucified.

Simon Peter: He was a fisherman, as were John and James, and these three formed the inner circle closest to Jesus. Jesus called Peter a "rock" and said "upon this rock I will build my church." After the arrest of Jesus, Peter denied him three times. Jesus personally commissioned him to "feed my sheep." Peter assumed the leadership of the Apostles. The Bible reports that he did many miracles. His ministry was mainly to the Jews, just as Paul's was to the Gentiles. He was a Judaizer until he received a vision and determined that "God is no respecter of persons....But in every nation he that feareth him, and worketh righteousness, is accepted with him (Acts 10:34-25)." However, pressure from Judaizers forced him to temporarily discontinue ministering to Gentiles. He wrote a letter (1st Epistle of Peter) while in Babylon. This "Babylon" may refer figuratively to Rome. It may also refer literally to Babylon in the Mesopotamia or Babylon in Egypt. There is a great possibility that he was in Babylon, Egypt, because he mentions that Mark was with him. Mark is the traditional bishop to Egypt and founder of the Coptic church. This Babylon was also called "Old Cairo," and served as the main communication network between Near East Asia and Lower Egypt.(6) It is widely believed that Peter also traveled to Rome, where he is traditionally considered the first bishop of Rome. It was in Rome that he was crucified around 64 A.D.

Simon, the Zealot: He and Judas Iscariot are the only disciples believed to be members of the Zealots, a revolutionary faction of Jews. According to *The Passion of Simon and Jude*, an apocryphal writing, Simon's ministry and martyrdom took place in Persia.

Thaddaeus: Also called Judas, son of James. Nothing is known of his post-resurrection activities.

Thomas: Popularly known as "Doubting Thomas" because of the doubts he had about the resurrection of Jesus. Tradition says he was a minister to Persia and southern India.

New Testament Authors

Matthew: See page 91. He wrote the book of Matthew sometime between 68 and 72 A.D.

Mark: Also called John Mark. The church in Jerusalem met in his mother's home. He was a close friend to Simon Peter. The second Gospel, the book of Mark, is believed to have been written by him as told to him by Peter. He traveled with Paul and Barnabas on their first missionary journey in 45 A.D.

93

During this journey, he left them in Perga and returned to Jerusalem, which greatly displeased Paul. It is believed that Mark was sent on his own missionary journey to take Christianity to Egypt where he is considered the founder of Egyptian Christianity and the first Bishop of Alexandria.(7) One tradition says Mark was killed in Alexandria.(8) He wrote the book of Mark between 40 and 68 A.D.

Luke: He was from Antioch and is identified as a physician. His authorship of the book of Luke and the Acts of the Apostles is widely accepted. These books were written to a gentile official named Theophilus. It is assumed that Luke was Greek because of his name and the type of Greek he used when translating Aramaic words. However, Paul refers to Luke twice in his writings and never identifies him as a Greek, as he certainly would have. Furthermore, Luke does not refer to himself as a Greek, which would have made his writings to Theophilus more personal, as one Gentile writing to another. He wrote the book of Luke and the Acts of the Apostles between 60 and 63 A.D.

John: See page 90. He wrote the Book of John around 80 A.D.; I John, II John and III John around 90 A.D.; and Revelations around 96 A.D.

Paul: See page 91. He wrote all of the letters credited to him between 52 A.D. to 67 A.D. The letters are Romans, I Corinthians, II Corinthians, Galatians, Ephesians, Philippians, Colossians, I Thessalonians, II Thessalonians, I Timothy, II Timothy, Titus, and Philemon.

James, the Lord's Brother: Also called "James the Just" and acknowledged by Paul as a "pillar of the church." He was a son of Mary and Joseph and the brother of Jesus. He did not accept the teachings of Jesus until after the resurrection. He quickly became a leader in the Christian movement as the head of the church in Jerusalem, the capital city of Christianity and Judaism. He was a devout Judaizer, but he also had the respect of Christians who believed converted Gentiles did not have to follow the Jewish laws. Pressure from the high priest and Sanhedrin led to the execution of James in 62 A.D. He was thrown from the Temple wall into a ravine, and then clubbed to death. His letters were written to the 12 tribes of Israel. He wrote the Epistle of James around 45 A.D.

Peter: See page 92. He wrote I Peter around 63 A.D. and II Peter around 66 A.D.

Jude: Also called Judas. He was the brother of Jesus and James. He is not to be confused with Judas Iscariot or the Apostle Judas. He wrote the Epistle of Jude around 80 A.D.

Disciples, Deacons and Believers

Apollos: By far, one of the most articulate and impressive leaders of the first century. He was an Egyptian Jew from Alexandria. He and others that traveled with him were disciples of John the Baptist. He arrived in Ephesus in 53 A.D. and taught in the synagogue. His teachings represented an excellent understanding of the Old Testament and the life of Jesus. He then traveled to Corinth where he attracted many people with his eloquent preaching. Some Corinthian Christians considered Apollos a rival of Paul, and factions developed between students of Apollos, Paul and Peter. Apollos later became the first bishop of Corinth.

Lucius of Cyrene: He was an African from Libya and important leader of the church in Antioch.

Philip the Evangelist: One of seven deacons chosen to distribute charity to the poor of Jerusalem. His ministry produced many miracles. Philip met the chief treasurer for the Queen of Ethiopia, who was reading the Old Testament scriptures in his chariot and related to him the teachings of Jesus.

Simeon Niger: The name "Niger" means black and is likely an indication of the region of Africa he came from. He was an important official in the Christian church in Antioch.

Simon of Cyrene: An African from Libya who carried the cross of Jesus to Golgotha. His sons, Alexander and Rufus, were well known among 1st century Christians.

Stephen: He was a Hellenized Jew and one of the seven deacons of Jerusalem. Stephen had a heated dispute with other Hellenized Jews that were members of the Synagogue of the Freedmen. Jews from Egypt and Asia Minor participated in this arguement, as well. This argument led to Stephen being charged with blasphemy, and later stoned to death.

NOTES

1) Rogers, J.A. *Sex and Race, Vol.III*, (Helga M. Rogers, St. Petersburg, FL 1944) p. 5.
2) deGraft-Johnson, J.C. *African Glory*, (Black Classic Press, Baltimore, MD 1986) p. 30.
3) Koester, Helmut. *History and Literature of Early Christianity*, (Walter DeGruyter, New York, NY 1987) p. 118.
4) Pamphilus, Eusebius. *Ecclesiastical History*, (Baker Book House, Grand Rapids, MI 1991) p. 82.
5) Comay, Joan and Ronald Brownrigg. *Who's Who in the Bible*, (Bonanza Books, New York, NY 1980) p. 152. and Pamphilus, *Ecclesiastical History*, p. 127.
6) Kamil, Jill. *Coptic Egypt History and Guide*, (The American University in Cairo Press, Cairo, Egypt 1987) p. 27.
7) Mbiti, John S. *Introduction to African Religion*, (Heinemann Educational Books, London, 1975) p. 182. and Conzelmann, Han. *History of Primitive Christianity*, (Abingdon Press, New York, 1973) p. 115.
8) Pearson, Birger A. and James E. Goehring, editors. *The Roots of Egyptian Christianity*, (Fortress Press, Philadelphia, PA 1986) p. 141.

CHAPTER 8

1ST CENTURY CHRISTIANITY IN AFRICA

The importance of Egypt to the life of Jesus is introduced early in the New Testament. According to Matthew 2:13-21, Joseph and Mary were divinely guided to take the newly born Jesus to Egypt to escape the wrath of Herod. A traditional site of Jesus' family is found in Old Cairo (called Babylon in the 1st century), where the Church of St. Sergius is located.(1) It is possible that Peter visited this "Babylon" and wrote his first letter while there.

The specific circumstances regarding the arrival of Christianity in Africa are not known. It is possible that the African Jews present at the day of Pentecost helped to spread the religion to their native lands.

The largest community of Jews outside of Palestine lived in Alexandria, Egypt. In fact, there were an estimated 200,000 Jews living in Alexandria and more than one million living throughout Lower (Northern) Egypt.(2) The Apostles began their mission by reaching Jewish communities through the synagogues of the Roman Empire. Because of the large Jewish communities in Egypt, and easy access between Palestine and Egypt, it is only natural that the Jews of Alexandria were among the first to be introduced to Christianity.(3) Adolf von Harnack, historian of Christianity, is quoted as saying, "It is more than a conjecture that a larger number of Jews were converted to Christianity in the Nile Valley than anywhere else."(4)

According to popular tradition Mark (John Mark, author of the second Gospel) was sent as a missionary to Egypt by the

Apostles, possibly around 41 A.D. Mark's visits to Alexandria are reported by Clement of Alexandria and Eusebius.(5) An extra-biblical writing called the *Acts of Mark* provides a more detailed account of Mark's activities. It reports that Mark first traveled to Cyrene (Libya), where he performed many miracles. He then went to Alexandria. The first person he met was a shoemaker named Annianus (or Ananias). While repairing Mark's sandal he injured his left hand and cried out, "God is One." Mark healed Annianus' hand and related to him the gospel of Jesus.(6) This account may be completely fictitious, however, Eusebius lists Annianus as the first bishop of Alexandria.

It is interesting and somewhat macabre to note that the head of Mark remains in the Cathedral of St. Mark in Alexandria. Other skeletal parts, called "relics," are kept in Latin churches in Venice, Italy, France, Belgium and Germany.(7)

The ministry of Apollos (reported in Acts 18:24), an Alexandrian Jew, during the apostolic period provides biblical proof that Christianity had began to spread in Alexandria during the first century. Birger A. Pearson, author of an article titled "Earliest Christianity in Egypt: Some Observations," printed in *The Roots of Egyptian Christianity*, states the following:

> It may nevertheless be interesting to note that the earliest documentable church, that of St. Theonas (bishop 282-300), lay in the northwestern part of the city, in the area we have identified as Delta, one of the "Jewish" quarters in the first century. This may imply a Jewish Christian presence in that area of the city before the time of the building of that

church, and that presence could have extended back to the first century. As has already been indicated, the earliest Christians would have lived side by side with other Jews, sharing the life of the synagogues and worshiping in house churches.(8)

Several factors contributed to the acceptance and growth of Christianity in Egypt during the 1st century. Despite almost 1000 years of foreign rule in Egypt, Egyptian culture and beliefs remained very strong. Instead of ending the Pharaonic rule of Egypt, foreign leaders assumed rulership as Pharaohs. They had great respect for Egyptian civilization and sought to emulate its greatness. One of the most important surviving aspects of Egyptian civilization was its mythology.

The most important characters in Egyptian mythology are Osiris, Isis and Horus. This trio of Egyptian mythology is of similar status to God, Mary and Jesus in Christian theology. A more detailed examination of this issue is provided in Chapter 9. Cosmogonical, theological and mythological beliefs already established in Egypt made this region fertile for the planting of Christianity.

Philo, a 1st century philosopher and Alexandrian Jew, reports the existence of a community of Egyptians called the "Therapeutae." Philo was born in Alexandria around 15 B.C. He was a contemporary of Jesus and was reported to have conversed with Peter in Rome sometime between 41 A.D. and 54 A.D. According to Eusebius, the name "Therapeutae" may refer to the curing or healing of "the souls of those that came to them, thus ridding them, like a physician, of disorders bred of evil."

101

Philo reports that the Therapeutoe (men of their community) and Therapeutrides (women of their community) were "exceedingly numerous in Egypt, in each of the nomes... and especially in the neighborhood of Alexandria." They renounced their property and moved to more solitary regions of the land. Each house in their communities had a sacred chamber, called the "holy place" or "monastery." In this room, an individual would bring no food, drink or anything for the body. The only items brought into the room were "laws, and inspired oracles from the lips of the prophets, and hymns and all else by which knowledge and piety are increased and perfected."(9) After dawn, they studied and meditated on sacred writings, "allegorizing the law of their fathers." Eusebius adamantly espoused the opinion that these Egyptian sects were early Christians. Probably before the title "Christians" was popularly used.

First century Christianity represents the infancy of a growing religion that was born in the small Galilee region of the vast Roman Empire. Early Christians were a mere nuisance to the Empire. They upset the Jewish leaders, refused to worship the emperor, refused to worship other gods, and sold their property, which deprived the Roman Empire from its right to tax them. They began as a Jewish sect with allegiance to Jerusalem. They soon became an independent religious sect, persecuted by Jewish leaders and the Roman government.

The new religion produced holy men, holy scriptures and holy prophesies. There were also heretics, forged scriptures and false religions associated with Christianity. The religion spread throughout the Empire and experienced its greatest success in Egypt. It was there that the religion was nurtured and grew

102

strong. Abraham went to Egypt a poor man and came out a wealthy man. Joseph entered Egypt a slave and became a great ruler. Jesus was taken into Egypt as a small baby and came out the "Son of God," fulfilling the words of the prophet Hosea, "Out of Egypt have I called my son."(Hosea 11:1 and Matthew 2:15)

Christianity started in Galilee, but it was established and made strong in Egypt. The Egyptian contributions to Christianity are many. The greatest of the church fathers were Africans; the first educational institution of the religion was in Egypt, started by an African; the monastic tradition began in Egypt, started by African men; the scriptures were translated and preserved for thousands of years in Egypt; and many of the ecumenical councils held to shape the future of the religion were influenced and controlled by Africans. For the first 400 years or more of Christianity, Africans played a pivotal role. The presence of black people in the Bible, and the shaping of Christianity, is not the exception, it is the rule. True biblical history cannot exist void of black people.

103

NOTES

1) Meinardus, Otto F.A. *Christian Egypt Ancient and Modern*, (The American University in Cairo Press,Cairo 1977) p. 1.
2) Groves, C.P. *The Planting of Christianity in Africa*, (Lutterworth Press, London 1948) p. 39.
3) Koester, Helmut. *History and Literature of Early Christianity*, (Walter De Gruyter, New York 1987) p. 220.
4) Groves, *The Planting of Christianity in Africa*, p. 36.
5) Pearson, Birger A. and James E. Goehring, Editors. *The Roots of Egyptian Christianity*, (Fortress Press, Philadelphia 1986) pp. 138-139 and
   Griggs, C. Wilfred. *Early Egyptian Christianity From Its Origins to 451 C.E.*, (E.J. Brill, New York 1990) pp. 19-21.
6) Pearson, *The Roots of Egyptian Christianity*, p. 140.
7) Meinardus, *Christian Egypt Ancient and Modern*, p. 28.
8) Pearson, *The Root of Egyptian Christianity*, pp. 151-152.
9) Pamphilus, Eusebius. *Ecclesiastical History*, (Baker Book House, Grand Rapids, MI 1991) pp. 49-50.

CHAPTER 9

CHRISTIAN AND EGYPTIAN BELIEFS COMPARED

For almost 2,000 years, Christian historians, theologians and ministers have frightfully avoided connecting Christianity with Egyptian beliefs. Many Christians believe that all Egyptian beliefs are false, evil, satanic, idolatrous and/or ungodly. It is natural to fear and hate what one does not understand. The connections between Christianity and Egyptian beliefs are blatantly obvious. To ignore these connections is like acknowledging a tree and joyfully eating its fruit, while simultaneously ignoring or hating its roots.

Early Christian theologians have been accused of stealing their theology from the Egyptians, the same as the Greeks stole philosophy from Egypt. Based on this charge, some historians reject Christianity as a false religion. This accusation is becoming more popular and causing many to look upon the religion suspiciously.

This chapter provides an examination of connections between Christian theology and certain Egyptian cosmogonies, mythologies and theologies. This text does not provide an exhaustive analysis of Egyptian belief, which would require many volumes of books. Instead, certain Christian theological beliefs are compared to ancient Egyptian beliefs.

For many years it was popularly believed that God created Adam and Eve about 5,000 years ago. This belief in a 5,000-year-old humanity has been rejected by modern theologians and scientists, placed in the same category as believing that the sun revolved around a flat earth. To acknowledge that humanity was created more than 5,000 years ago is the first step toward

105

understanding the continuity of beliefs from Egyptian to Christian.

Scientists estimate human lineage began more than 2.5 million years ago in Africa with a species called "Homo habilis." They believe that the first "modern humans" existed between 100,000 to 200,000 years ago.(1) Biblical history begins about 5,000 years ago with no references to humanity existing before Adam. It must be concluded that belief in a 5,000-year-old humanity is in error. The dismissal of this belief produces a question; that is, "How was the Creator (or God) viewed by humans more than 5,000 years ago?"

It is not possible to know all of the religions that have existed since the creating of humanity. However, the beliefs held by the ancient Egyptians are made known to us through the histories recorded in the pyramids, papyrus records and popular myths. These beliefs pre-date Christianity by more than 5,000 years, and remained popular in Egypt into the 4th century. According to Saint Augustine, "It must be confessed that before Moses there had already been, not indeed among the Greeks, but among the barbarous nations, as in Egypt, some doctrine which might be called their wisdom, else it would not have been written in the holy books that Moses was learned in all the wisdom of the Egyptians."(2)

The biblical creation account, presumably written by Moses, begins with the eternal God's creating of the earth, making it "without form, and void," somehow composed of "waters." God then created light, separated the waters with a firmament (or atmosphere), formed the earth land masses, created various life forms and then created man. This is somewhat similar to ancient Egyptian cosmogony, which taught the eternal existence of primordial matter that was not created. This matter was called "Nun." Somehow, Nun became self-aware and began to bring the mass of primordial matter into order, creating the world. At this point the Nun becomes "Ra," the first God.(3) The first creations of Ra were four divine pairs. These pairs were Shu and Tefnut or air and humidity; Geb and Nut or earth and heaven; Osiris and Isis, the fertile human couple to beget humanity; and Seth and Nephthys, the infertile couple that would bring evil to humanity.

According to John 1:1, it was through the "Word," that was "with God" and "was God," that all things were made. Similarly, it was through the "Ka" (universal reason) that Ra created the world. The use of Ka in Egyptian cosmogony is equivalent to the use of the "logos" (Greek for Word) in this scripture.

So far, the God of Egyptian cosmogony is represented in three different forms. These forms are the Nun, Ra and Ka. The Egyptians interpreted these and other representations as distinct and different aspects of the one Supreme God. In Genesis, God is quoted as saying "Let us make man...." This use of "us" obviously implies more than one. It could be compared to the many aspects of God, referred to by the Egyptians as the Netcherw collectively or Netcher individually. The word nature is derived from this word. It has been translated to mean "god-like," "holy," "divine," "sacred," "power," "strength," "force," "strong," "fortify," "mighty," and "protect."(4)

In Genesis, the making of man out of dust, and the words of Isaiah 64:8, "We are the clay, and thou our potter," are often compared to the making of man by the Netcher Khunum. Thousands of years before the writing of Genesis, Khunum was portrayed sitting at a potter's table forming man. The murder of Abel by Cain in Genesis can be compared to the murder of Osiris, by his jealous brother Seth.

The Egyptians believed that there were certain truths that could not be explained through simple sciences and history. These truths represent Egyptian sciences, histories, religions, mathematics, philosophies and spirituality. The myths were developed to represent these truths and to express complicated belief systems. Many cultures use allegories and metaphors to express certain ideas. The use of myths were the highest form of this expression of ideas.

Over thousands of years, popular *Osirian* myths developed in Egypt. The myths are variations of the same general story. According to the myth, Osiris was the fertile man created by Ra. His infertile brother, Seth, became jealous of him and plotted to kill him. Through trickery, Seth trapped Osiris inside a chest and threw him into the Nile River. The chest was later found by Isis, the wife of Osiris. When Seth realized that the body of Osiris was found, he was able to recapture it, cut it into 14 pieces, and scatter them across the land. Isis was able to recover 13 of the pieces.

Isis was given certain words by the Netcher Thoth. Thoth represents divine articulation of speech and truth. When Isis spoke these words to the dismembered body of Osiris, she received the seed of Osiris and became pregnant, giving birth to Horus. This conception is the oldest story of a virgin birth in history. For this reason, Horus was mocked and considered deformed because he was born of the seed of someone who was dead. The incantations spoken by Isis led to the resurrection of Osiris, who ultimately became the judge of the departed souls, seated on the Throne of Judgement. The same as Jesus serving as "judge" of "the living and dead," as stated in the Apostle's Creed.

When Horus matured, he had many battles with Seth to avenge the murder of his father. Horus became the victor over Seth and represents the triumph of good over evil.(5)

It was this ancient Osirian myth that was taught to Moses (Acts 7:22), and later told to Alexander "the Great" more than 300 years before the Christian era.(6) As a people from Egypt, the Israelites were well acquainted with the worship of Isis and the Osirian myths. According to Jill Kamil, author of *Coptic Egypt History and Guide*, "The cult of Egypt's most beloved goddess Isis exerted a strong influence on the early church, and particularly on Coptic Christianity."(7)

When comparing the life of Jesus with that of Horus, we learn that both were born of a virgin, baptized at the age of 30, share December 25th as a birthdate, and each are referred to as "the Son of God." Portrayals of an infant Horus in the arms of his mother are the earliest forms of a madonna and child, and pre-date Jesus by more than 3,000 years. Osiris and Jesus are similar in that both were violently killed and then resurrected, and both are characterized as God judging the souls of humanity.

In Revelations 3:14 Jesus is called the "Amen, the faithful and true witness, the beginning of the creation of God." In Egyptian cosmogonies, Amen is the Netcher used by Ra to create the other Netcherw.

There are also commonalities between Seth (also Set or Seti) and Satan. They both represent all that is evil and against the nature of God.

109

Long before the Christian era, the Egyptians believed in one true and supreme God, the creation of humanity, resurrection of the body, life after physical death, the judging of the soul, the virgin birth, and the victory of good over evil. They also lived according to certain laws called the *Declarations of Innocence* or *Admonitions of Maat.* The Declarations were composed of more than 147 negative confessions, which were learned by the Egyptians in preparation for their day of judgement before Osiris. On that day, the deceased would declare "I have not stolen," "I have done no murder," "I have not spoken lies," "I have not committed fornication," "I have not defiled the wife of any other man," and so on. These negative confessions pre-date the Ten Commandments by thousands of years.(8)

Even if early Christians in Palestine were completely unaware of Egyptian beliefs, the Jews and Christians of Egypt were completely aware of the myths. The Greeks and Romans adopted the Egyptian myths and fashioned their gods according to certain Netcherw.

It is likely that Egyptian beliefs influenced the developing of the Christian religion. The similarities may have developed naturally because the Israelites were originally from Egypt. Early Christians may have taken from Egyptian beliefs and claimed them as their own. The similarities may be expressions of the same God and beliefs as experienced by two different cultures. In any case, the beliefs represent a truth far greater than any religion.

NOTES

1) *Newsweek*, "The Search for Adam and Eve" by John Tierney, January 11, 1988, pp. 46-52 and
   U.S. News and World Report, "Who We Were" by William F. Allman, September 16, 1991, pp. 53-60.
2) Saint Augustine. *The City of God*, (The Modern Library of Random House, New York, NY 1950) p. 646.
3) Diop, Cheikh Anta. *Civilization or Barbarism*, (Lawrence Hill Books, Brooklyn, NY 1991) pp. 310-311.
4) Budge, E.A. Wallis. *The Book of the Dead*, (Universal Books, Inc. Secaucus, NJ 1960) pp. 99-100   and
   Browder, Anthony T. *Nile Valley Contributions to Civilization*, (The Institute of Karmic Guidance, Washington D.C. 1992) p. 83.
5) Ibid., p. 89   and
   Kamil, Jill. *Coptic Egypt History and Guide*, (The American University in Cairo Press, Cairo, Egypt 1987) p. 30.
6) Augustine, *The City of God*, p. 279.
7) Kamil, *Coptic Egypt History and Guide*, p. 29.
8) Saakana, Amon Saba, Editor. *The Afrikan Origin of the Major World Religions*, (Karnak House 1988) pp. 25-26.

CHAPTER 10

FATHERS OF THE CHRISTIAN CHURCH

During the 1st century, the apostles and their disciples facilitated the spread of Christianity. As these apostolic fathers passed on, Christianity continued to grow and change. A Zealot-led rebellion against the Romans resulted in the total destruction of Jerusalem in 70 A.D. and Antioch became the primary center for Christianity in Palestine. Christians suffered periods of persecution under different Emperors for almost 400 years and church meetings were often held in secret. The growth of Christianity did not happen with the support of the Roman government. It grew in spite of often brutal Roman opposition. Despite the New Testament emphasis on European and Palestinian Christian communities, it was in North Africa that Christianity truly matured. The Roman church made very few, if any, significant contribution to early Christianity.

The development of the Christian church after the 1st century was largely guided by certain men. The contributions of these men to Christian theology, history and practices are invaluable. They have earned the recognition of the Christian world as the Fathers of the Christian Church and most of them were Africans.

The eight black men presented in this chapter were not the only Africans to influence the development of Christianity, but they are among the most notable church fathers. Their names are Basilides, Valentinus, Pantaenus, Tertullian, Origen, Cyprian, Athanasius and Augustine. These men are held in high esteem in Christian history. However, their heritage as Africans is usually omitted from the historical record. Like most biblical figures, they are often falsely portrayed as white.

Historical documentation verifying their race differs from one person to the next. Criteria used to conclude that they were black men include: 1) being born in Africa 2) born of African parents 3) wrote and spoke non-European languages 4) acknowledged their African heritage in their own writings 5) called African by other writers or 6) had names that reflect African beliefs.

Basilides

He was an Alexandrian Christian teacher during the earlier part of the 2nd century (around 125 A.D.), and claimed an apostolic succession through the apostle Matthias.(1) He was the first to write a commentary on the gospels and the founder of the first school of gnostic Christianity in Alexandria. Gnostics taught that those initiated into its mysteries gained salvation through special knowledge (*gnosis* in Greek) revealed by a spiritual savior.

Basilides taught that divine life unfolds in seven successive stages and that man has two souls, one rational trying to dominate the other one, which is animal or material. He also believed that a "nonexistent God" produced a "nonexistent seed," and from this seed "existent things" were produced. One of the existent things produced was a "threefold Sonship" whose goal was to return to the nonexistent God.(2) Salvation would be achieved when the Sonship is brought into eternal rest in its proper position. These beliefs were classified as heretical. However, they were accepted by many early Christians and the presence of followers of Basilides continued into the 4th century A.D.

114

Valentinus

He was a gnostic teacher and poet born in Egypt and probably educated in Alexandria. He taught in Egypt before traveling to Rome around 140 A.D. Only fragments of his writings remain. However, it is possible that he is the author of the *Gospel of Truth*, one of the books found near Nag Hammadi in Upper Egypt. The gnostic schools founded by him are considered more impressive than that of his predecessor, Basilides.

Valentinus taught that Jesus shared knowledge with the disciples that he did not share with the masses, consistent with the words of Jesus presented in the New Testament, "Unto you it is given to know the mysteries of the kingdom of God: but to others in parables; that seeing they may not see, and hearing they may not understand."(3) These mysteries were taught to certain believers by the apostles and their students. Valentinus claimed that he learned the mysteries from Theudas, a student of Paul.

He also taught that there were three classes of human beings. The highest form of human was pneumatikoi, a spiritual person; the second was psychikoi, one that merely possesses a soul; and the lowest form was hylikoi, one that was only matter and void of spirit or soul.(4) The most notable student of Valentinus was Origen and Valentinians were present into the 4th century.

Pantaenus (150 to 220 A.D.)

He was the founder and first head of the *Didascalia*, the world-famous Catechetical School in Alexandria. It was the first educational center established to instruct its students in proper

115

orthodox Christian theology. As the most well known and highly respected institution of Christian thought, it had no rival. Eusebius describes Pantaenus as "one of the most eminent teachers of his day" and a stoic philosopher. His teaching was so eloquent that he was sent to India to preach the gospel to the people of the East.(5) The brilliance of his lectures attracted many students, including Clements of Alexandria, another great church father.

Tertullian (155 to 245 A.D.)

His full name was Quintus Septimius Florens Tertullian. He was born in Carthage and trained as a lawyer. Around 198 A.D., while practicing law in Rome, he became a Christian and moved back to Carthage. Shortly after returning home, he was made a presbyter. Eusebius called him "one of the most brilliant men in Rome."(6)

Tertullian was the first to popularize the use of Latin in writing Christian literature and Harnack stated that "Tertullian in fact created Christian Latin literature....Cyprian polished the language...Augustine, again, stood on the shoulders of Tertullian and Cyprian these three North Africans are the fathers of the Western Churches."(7) His many writings were systematic, precise and polemical. Around 203 he became a Montanist. The Montanists expected the return of Jesus during their time. They lived strict and disciplined lives of prayer, fasting, celibacy and regarded martyrdom as a most honorable service. Tertullian was the most notable Montanist convert.

The decision of Callistus, the Bishop of Rome, to absolve and remit the sins of penitent adulterers and fornicators caused a great deal of controversy. Tertullian taught that there were seven unforgivable sins that would exclude Christians from the church without the possibility of re-admission. These sins were murder, idolatry, theft, apostasy, blasphemy, fornication and adultery. He believed that Callistus' decision lowered church standards.(8) The decision of Callistus was ultimately accepted by the church over the objections of Tertullian.

Other theological issues expounded on and popularized by Tertullian include the trinity of the Father (God), Son (Jesus) and the Holy Spirit; baptism; the Lord's Prayer; forms of worship; and repentance. He explained his Christian beliefs with this paradox, "The Son of God was born, I am not ashamed of it because it is shameful; the Son of God died, it is credible for the very reason that it is silly; and, having been buried, he rose again, it is certain because it is impossible."(9)

Origen (186 to 255 A.D.)

Also called Origines Adametius, he was born in Alexandria and became a very serious and famous Christian writer and teacher. The name "Origen" is derived from the Egyptian god Horus and may indicate that he was born on the anniversary of Horus.(10)

As a child his family lived under the rule of the Emperor Septimius Severus, who was also an African. Origen was trained in the scriptures by his father, Leonides. A great love for the Christian faith was nurtured in him by his father's teachings. Severus made laws forbidding Christians and Jews from making new converts. Leonides was arrested and subsequently martyred for violating these laws.

Origen was close to 16 when his father was killed. Eusebius described him as having "an ambition extraordinary in one so young" and "an enthusiasm beyond his years."(11) The martyrdom of his father greatly effected him. He longed for the opportunity to give his life for the cause of Christ and often placed himself in situations that would have naturally led to him being stoned to death. However, he was always miraculously saved from death. His fearlessness encouraged thousands of Christians to boldly face martyrdom.

He became the most brilliant student of Clement at the Catechetical School in Alexandria and succeeded Clement as the head of the school. Origen subjected himself to extreme methods of discipline, which included long periods of fasting, sleep deprivation and poverty. His most extreme action was self mutilation. Heeding the words of Matthew that "there be eunuchs, which made themselves eunuchs for the kingdom of heaven's sake"(Matthew 19:12), Origen cut off his penis.

Because of his zeal and expertise in Christian theology, his fame spread throughout the Christian world. He was invited to Arabia and Palestine to lecture. About 215 A.D. he spoke at the church in Caesarea. It was rare for a layman to be invited to speak in a church, as this honor was usually given to ordained clerics. His speaking in the church displeased Demetrius, the Bishop of Alexandria. Origen was promptly ordered to return to Alexandria, where he continued to teach for 15 years. Around 232 A.D. he left Alexandria and was made a presbyter by the Bishops of Caesarea. His rise as an ordained minister was opposed by Demetrius, who held a meeting of bishops and they rejected the ordaining of Origen because of his act of self-mutilation.(12)

Neither the opposition of Demetrius or the persecution of Severus broke the spirit and will of Origen, who continued to serve the church and grow in fame. He traveled for several years and then settled in Caesarea, where he established a second catechetical school. Many of the students trained by him became high church officials an theologians.

His writings include a commentary on the book of *John*, *De Principiis*, *Homilies*, *Of Origins*, *On Martyrdom*, and his *Hexapla*. The *Hexapla* presented the Old Testament in the original Hebrew with a Greek transliteration, a Greek version of the Septuagint, Aquila, Symmachus and Theodotion, all arranged in six parallel columns.

In 249 A.D. Origen was tortured under the persecution of the Emperor Decius. He survived this torture and lived for six more years before dying in 255 A.D. Harnack is quoted as saying that "all thinkers were under his influence" in the Christian world of the 4th century.(13)

In later years, some of the teachings of Origen were declared heretical. Augustine challenged Origen's opinion of the nature of sin and reincarnation presented in *Of Origins*.(14) His doctrines became increasingly viewed as more controversial during the Middle Ages.

Cyprian (200 to 258 A.D.)

Also called Thascius Caecilius Cyprianus. Little is known of his early years. The historical accounts regarding him begin around 240 A.D. At that time he was a Carthaginian land owner and trained in Roman law. He had a reputation of being an excellent orator. When he became a Christian, he sold his material goods and gave the money to the poor, which was an act popular among the apostles and many early Christians. In 249 A.D. he was ordained a presbyter and shortly after replaced

Donatus as the Bishop of Carthage.(15)

From 250 to 251 A.D. the persecution of the Emperor Decius forced him into exile and he continued to guide his church by correspondence. When he returned, he was confronted with a controversy regarding the *lapsi*. The lapsi were those Christians who rejected their faith during the persecution and many of them wanted to be re-admitted into the church. The issue produced two opposing parties. One group favored lax treatment of the lapsi and another that demanded severe treatment. Cyprian insisted on an act of penance from the lapsi, before the possibility of absolution would be allowed. This approach didn't satisfy either party and the matter was never completely settled.

The controversy continued and expanded when the presbyter Novatianus, the leader of those who wanted the lapsi to be treated severely, opposed the appointment of Cornelius as the Bishop of Rome. Cyprian supported the appointment. Cornelius served for three years and was succeeded by Lucius, who died after eight months as bishop.

In 254 A.D. Cyprian was at odds with Stephen, the successor of Lucius as the bishop of Rome. The issue was whether baptism administered to someone by one declared a heretic was valid. Stephen, along with other church leaders in Rome and Alexandria, considered the baptisms valid as long as water was used and the candidate followed the proper rituals. According to Tertullian, these rituals included prayer, fasting and an all-night vigil the day before the rite; confession of all sins; a repudiation of Satan and his angels; an anointing with oil; the taking of milk and honey; three immersions into the water; and a confession of faith in God, Jesus and the Holy Spirit. Cyprian argued that a person baptized by a heretic must be baptized again, while Stephen upheld the tradition of prayer and a "laying on of hands" of these Christians.(16)

In 256 A.D. Cyprian became involved in another issue that would not be settled until long after his death and would greatly effect the future of the Christian world. It was the question of Roman judicial authority over other bishops. From the 1st to the 4th century, there were three main centers of Christianity. They were Alexandria in Egypt, Antioch in Syria, and Rome in Italy. The bishops of these cities were more powerful then those of smaller sees and began to exert power over them.

Cyprian challenged the power of the Bishop of Rome over other sees. He argued that episcopal authority originated with Jesus, who first passed it to Peter and then to the other Apostles. This authority was then passed on by the Apostles to their students, who continued to pass it on over the years. This same authority was shared equally by all bishops, according to Cyprian and was not the sole property of any particular bishop.(17) Therefore, the unity of the church rested in this shared authority, and all people outside of the church were not true Christians. In later years the supremacy of the See of Rome was forced on the Christian world by authority of the Roman government.

The persecution of Christians was renewed in 257 A.D. by Emperor Valerian. Cyprian bravely accepted martyrdom on September 14, 258 A.D. Before being beheaded he thanked those who sentenced him to death, and gave 25 pieces of gold to his executioner.(18)

Athanasius (293 to 373 A.D.)

He was born in Upper Egypt and raised by his parent for church service. He rose through the ranks of church leadership to become Bishop of Alexandria in 319 A.D. He chose to spend much of the first six years of his episcopate among the monastic circles, and Christian communities of the desert regents along the Nile River and Libyan border.

His 47 years as bishop started with a controversy that began with his predecessor, Alexander. The matter was initiated by an Egyptian presbyter named Arius. Arius challenged the opinion of Origen that the Son of God was of a "eternal, timeless generation." Arius argued that a generation cannot be "timeless" and that there must have been a point when the generation of Christ began. Athanasius held that if the Son was not eternal, he was subject to change. This nature of being subject to change makes Christ inconsistent and the possibility of eternal salvation unstable. This issue became known as the Arian controversy, and it led to the Council of Nicea in 325 A.D.

The Council of Nicea upheld the opinion of Athanasius, which resulted in the establishing of the *Nicene Creed*. Yet, the controversy was far from over. Arius used his political connections with the Roman government, which began a period of toleration of Christianity in 313 A.D. to hold another council meeting in Tyre in 335 A.D. The council was dominated by supporters of Arian and had the enforcement of Emperor Constantine. It resulted in Athanasius being deposed as bishop and banished to Gaul for three years. This was the first of five exiles that Anthanasius suffered from 335 to 363 A.D., because of this controversy. Christian history recognizes him as the

"Father of Orthodoxy."

Athanasius was a prolific writer and provided the first listing of the 27 New Testament books (Matthew though Revelation), as they occur in the present canon of the Bible. He also issued an order purging all heretical writings.(19) He wrote *The Life of St. Antony* in 357 A.D., which spread throughout the Christian world and greatly inspired many people.

Augustine (354 to 430 A.D.)

Also called Aurelius Augustinus. He is regarded as the greatest of the Fathers of the Church and served as the Bishop of Hippo in Africa. He was born in Tagaste, Numidia, and was educated in Madaura (not far from Tagaste) and Carthage. As a young man he studied astrology, Aristotle, Plato, neoplatonism and skepticism. He had great appreciation for the Latin language, which he accepted as a second language, but considered Greek difficult and too foreign.(20) While rejecting Christianity, he became a member of the Manicheans, a North African sect of Gnosticism that taught a form of radical dualism.

He first taught in Tagaste, where he started his family, and then in Carthage before moving to teach in Rome at the age of 29 in 383 A.D. He soon learned of a position in Milan as Master of Rhetoric. Milan had replaced Rome as the new center for imperial government. Augustine succeeded in gaining this position over several other candidates. It was in Milan that he met St. Ambrose and ultimately became a Christian.

While struggling to overcome an overactive sex drive, Augustine sought solitude in a quiet garden, where he heard a child's voice say "take, read." There he found a copy of Paul's

Letter to the Romans, and read in the 13th chapter "not in rioting and drunkenness, not in chambering and wantonness, not in strife and envying, but put ye on the Lord Jesus Christ, and make not provision for the flesh, to fulfil the flesh thereof."(21) In addition to his conversion experience, his acceptance of Christianity was also influenced by his mother, a highly spiritual Christian woman. She visited him in Italy after his conversion and was proud of his accomplishments. His mother died while returning to Africa and his joy turned to pain.

Augustine returned to Africa, intending to start a monastery. However, he was immediately and aggressively entreated to accept the position of Bishop of Hippo in North Africa. He accepted this church office in 395 A.D.

Pelaguis, a British monk, initiated one of the first church controversies that Augustine participated in. Pelaguis taught that eternal life could be gained without the grace of God provided through Jesus if a person lived a "stainless" life. This teaching violated an orthodox belief in the "original sin," which was first stated by Paul in Romans 5:12. It was commonly believed that sin entered humanity through the disobedience of Adam and Eve. This original sin was passed on to all humanity and forgiven by the grace of God given through Jesus. Augustine led the fight against Pelaguis' heresy, which was condemned by the Council of Ephesus. Augustine's success in this matter earned him recognition as the "Doctor of Grace."(22)

He also gained respect in his challenge to the Arians and Manichaeans. His voluminous writings included 93 major works, 263 sermons and 260 letters. His two most revered and celebrated writings are his *Confessions*, an autobiography of his struggles for conversion, and *The City of God*, a theological explanation for historical events. Through his writings, he defended Christianity against those who blamed the religion for the fall of the Roman Empire. In his *Expositions of the Psalms*, he eloquently encouraged Christians in their duty to each other with these words: "The man you cannot put right is still yours. He is part of you; either as a fellow human being, or very often as a member of your church, he is inside with you....Strive humbly to be what you would have him be, and you will not think that he is what you are not."(23)

In 410 A.D. Rome was invaded by the barbaric Goths, led by Alaric, an Arian Christian. The siege produced great hunger in Rome and some people resorted to cannibalism to survive. Jerome, a Palestinian monk, reports the desperation of the Romans in his letter titled *Jerome to Principia*, where he writes "The rage of hunger had recourse to impious food; men tore one another's limbs, and the mother did not spare the baby at her breast, taking again within her body that which her body had just brought forth."(24)

In 429 A.D. the Vandals invaded North Africa. Like the Goths, the Vandals were Gothic-speaking Arian Christians with white skin and blond hair. They focused much of their attention on destroying churches, basilicas, cemeteries, monasteries and houses of prayer. Augustine died in 430 from an illness while Hippo remained under siege until 439 A.D.

NOTES

1) Grant, Robert M. *Second-Century Christianity*, (The Trustees of the Society for Promoting Christian Knowledge, London, 1957) p. 19.

2) Grant, Robert M. *Augustus to Constantine*, (Harper & Row, Publishers, New York, NY 1970) p. 125   and
Koester, Helmut, *History and Literature of Early Christianity*, (Walter De Gruyter, New York, NY 1987) p. 232.

3) Pagels, Elaine. *The Gnostic Gospels*, (Random House, New York, NY 1979) P. 14   and
The Original African Heritage Study Bible, King James Version, (James C. Winston Publishing Company, Nashville, TN. 1993) Luke 8:10.

4) Koester, *History and Literature of Early Christianity*, p. 233.

5) Williamson, G.A. Translator. *Eusebius The History of the Church from Christ to Constantine*, (Augsburg Publishing House, Minneapolis, MN 1965) p. 213.

6) Ibid., p. 75.

7) Ayerst, David and A.S.T. Fisher. *Records of Christianity*, (Basil Blackwell, Oxford) pp. 94-95.

8) Beven, Edwyn. *Christianity*, (Oxford University Press, London, 1932) pp. 78-79.

9) Ayerst, *Records of Christianity*, p. 95.

10) Oulton, John Ernest Leonard and Henry Chadwick, Translators. *Alexandrian Christianity*, (The Westminster Press, Philadelphia, PA) p. 171.

11) Williamson, *Eusebius The History of the Church from Christ to Constantine*, pp. 240,244.

12) Oulton, *Alexandrian Christianity*, pp. 175-176.
13) Beven, *Christianity*, p. 77.
14) Saint Augustine. *The City of God*, (The Modern Library of Random House, New York, NY 1950) pp. 366-368.
15) Clarke, G.W., Translator. *The Letters of St. Cyprian of Carthage*, (Newman Press, New York, NY 1950) pp. 14-15.
16) Latourette, Kenneth Scott. *A History of Christianity Vol.I*, (Harper & Row Publishers, New York, NY 1975) pp. 194-196 and

  Williamson, *Eusebius The History of the Church from Christ to Constantine*, p. 288.

          217) Beven, *Christianity*, p. 112   and
  Latourette, *A History of Christianity Vol.I*, p. 133.
18) deGraft-Johnson, J.C. *African Glory*, (Black Classic Press, Baltimore, MD 1954) p. 42.
19) Pagels, *The Gnostic Gospels*, p. 120.
20) degraft-Johnson, *African Glory*, p. 44.
21) Latourette, *A History of Christianity Vol.I*, pp. 96-97.
22) Harney, Martin P. *The Catholic Church Through the Ages*, (Daughters of St. Paul, Boston, MA 1974) pp. 61-62.
23) Ayerst, *Records of Christianity*, p. 288.
24) Ibid., p. 295.

CHAPTER 11

CHRISTIAN EDUCATION

In Alexandria, Egypt, the first institution of Christian education was established sometime around 180 A.D. by Pantaenus. It was called the Didascalia or Catechetical School. As these names imply, it provided a didactical method of presenting Christian theology to its catechumens (students being prepared for church membership). In addition to theology, the students studied philosophy and literature. They also copied scriptural manuscripts for distribution throughout the Christian world.(1) The school probably began with Pantaenus attracting a small group of young men with his teachings, but it grew to be the greatest institution for Christian education of its time.

When Pantaenus died around 200 A.D., Clement of Alexandria became the next head of the Didascalia. He was one of Pantaenus' best students, but little is known of his short tenure as head of the school. It is believed that he was born in Athens around 150 A.D. and came to Alexandria around 180 A.D. Clement left Egypt around 203 A.D. to escape a period of persecution started by Septimus Severus. He went on to become a great theologian and writer.

The next to head the school was Origen, a 17 year old who studied under Pantaenus and Clement. Demetrius, the Bishop of Alexandria, appointed Origen as head of the school because of his reputation of being precocious, a very competent teacher and zealous in spite of the persecuting of Christians. The school grew in quality and quantity, teaching men and women under the leadership of Origen.(2) His fame spread throughout the Christian world and he was often invited to teach abroad.

Around 231 A.D., Origen resigned his position as head of the Didascalia. The reason for his departure was most likely due to increasing conflicts with Demetrius. He continued to serve the church while living in Caesarea in Palestine, and also started another catechetical school there.

Origen was succeeded by his best student, Heracles, who shortly thereafter replaced Demetrius when he died in 231 A.D. as Bishop of Alexandria. Heracles was responsible for teaching the lower level students, while Origen taught the more advanced students. Eusebius described Heracles as "a remarkable example of the philosophic (ascetic) life and discipline."(3)

Leadership of the Didascalia was then gained by another of Origen's best students, Dionysius of Alexandria. He continued as head of the school until 248 A.D. when he became Bishop of Alexandria. Little is known about the history of the school after Dionysius. It continued beyond the 4th century and heads of the school included Theognostus, Prierus, Achillas and Peter of Alexandria.

Though the Didascalia was not like the large, modern Christian institutions of today, it produced the greatest Christian theologians in history.

NOTES

1) Meinardus, Otto F.A. *Christian Egypt Ancient and Modern*, (The American University in Cairo, 1977) p. 4.
2) Oulton, John Ernest Leonard and Henry Chadwick, Translators. *Alexandrian Christianity*, (The Westminster Press, Philadelphia) pp. 173-174.
3) Williamson, G.A. Translator. *Eusebius The History of the Church From Christ to Constantine*, (Augsburg Publishing House, Minneapolis, MN 1965) p. 242.

CHAPTER 12

CHRISTIAN MONASTICISM

The word "monk" seldom evokes the image of an African man living a life of prayer, solitude and service. However, the monastic tradition has its deepest roots in the sands of the Egyptian deserts. The ascetic lifestyle had its origin in Egypt long before the founding of Christian monasticism.

The three basic kinds of monastic lifestyles are the eremite, the eremitic community and the cenobitic. The eremite lived as a hermit away from other people, completely committed to the ascetic life. Those of the eremitic community lived in individual dwellings near other hermits. Those of the cenobitic community lived together in a monastery and their ascetic living was guided by a head monk.

There are two black men and one black woman who deserve the credit as founders of Christian monasticism. First is St. Antony, who was the first Christian known to live as a eremite and to form a eremitic community. The second is Pachomius, who instituted the cenobitic form of monastic living that became known as Pachomian Monasticism. Mary, the sister of Pachomius, founded the first nunneries (or convents) of Christianity.

The contributions of the Christian monasteries of Africa to Christianity cannot be overstated. They set the pace for monasticism throughout the world. They translated and preserved scriptural documents and they provided living examples of lives totally committed to God through Christ.

Antony was born of Christian parents around 250 A.D. in Coma in Middle Egypt. His parents died around 269 A.D., leaving him their wealth and the responsibility as guardian of a younger sister. Several months later, Antony's life was changed when he heard the story of the young wealthy man told by Jesus: "If thou wilt be perfect, go and sell that thou hast, and give to the poor, and thou shalt have treasures in heaven: and come and follow me." (Matthew 19:21) Unlike the young man in the story, Antony accepted this challenge to become perfect. He sold all of his wealth, distributed his property among the people of his town, and gave his money to the poor.(1)

He placed his sister in the care of the women of his community and moved into the desert to live the ascetic life. Antony learned from other Egyptian men who already were living the ascetic life and applied biblical concepts to this ancient Egyptian practice. He lived a life of prayer, fasting and manual labor. Antony was about 20 years old when he had a friend lock him inside a vault of tombs, bringing him bread and water from time to time. He stayed there for 15 years, learning to resist temptation and being attacked by demons. While there, he received a vision from God telling him that he would always be by his side and that Antony would be world renown.

Antony then moved to a desert fort at Pispir, Egypt, where he lived for 20 years. This became his "Outer Mountain." There were many people who came to him to receive guidance on how they could live the monastic life. They were inspired by his life of sacrifice, amazed by miracles performed by him and divinely moved by his preaching about the love of Christ. He became the leader and teacher of those who came to live the monastic life at Pispir. When he wanted to be alone, he travelled further into the desert toward the Red Sea, where he found a spring and date palms. This was his "Inner Mountain." He grew a small garden there and this was his place of personal prayer and meditation.

He presented teachings on the vocation of the monk, the power of prayer over Satan, gifts of the spirit and discerning good and evil spirits.(2) He strongly opposed Arianism and denounced their views. He led a group of monks to Alexandria to minister to persecuted Christians and hoped that he would be martyred while there. Upon returning from Alexandria, he increased his acts of self-sacrifice by fasting more, giving up bathing and wearing a hair shirt (worn with the animal hairs against the skin to cause discomfort).

He continued to grow in fame. In addition to providing counsel to fellow African Christians, he also counseled Emperor Constantine and two of his sons.(3) As he reached the end of his life, he finally retreated to his "Inner Mountain" and died in 356 A.D. at the age of 105. His fame spread further throughout the world after his death, through an autobiography on his life written by Athanasius, the Bishop of Alexandria.

Pachomius was born around 285 A.D. in Upper Egypt. He was recruited into the Roman army, stationed at Thebes and also served a prison sentence. When he was released from prison around 320 A.D. he became a Christian and was baptized by an eremite named Palomen. He remained a student of Palomen until he received a vision, which led him and several other disciples of Palomen to establish their own community near Ahkmim. Pachomius attracted many eremites to their community and began to guide their spiritual journeys. He scheduled their daily lives, prescribing times for sleep, prayer, eating and work.(4)

For anyone seeking to join the Pachomian monastery, they had to complete a probationary period before being given a habit (clothing worn by the monk), and being accepted as a member of the community.

Pachomius founded more than 11 monasteries in Upper Egypt. Each monastery held as many as 300 monks and was surrounded by a wall. There were houses within the walls, and each house had individual cells for 20 to 40 monks. Each house also had a church, meeting room, kitchen, dining room, library and infirmary.(5) Daily life in a Pachomian monastery consisted of daily prayer, Eucharist (taking of bread and wine to symbolize the body of Christ) twice a week, sleeping in a sitting position, memorization of scriptures, manual labor, two meals a day (no meats or wine were allowed), community fasting twice a week, chastity, and poverty.

Mary, Pachomius' sister, founded the first Christian nunnery or convent. Though they were an official part of Pachomian monasticism, the men and women were kept separate.

Pachomius died in a plague in 346 A.D. Despite internal conflicts about leadership of the monasteries, the Pachomian monastic form spread throughout the world. There is no doubt that the monks and nuns of the world owe a debt of respect to Antony, Pachomius and Mary.

The monasteries of Egypt were well known and respected throughout the world. According to Jill Kamil, author of *Coptic Egypt History and Guide*, "Pilgrims came from all over the Christian world to visit the monasteries of Egypt." Ten thousand monks met at Arsinoe in the Fayoum at the end of the 5th century. At the beginning of the 6th century, there were more than 10,000 monks and 20,000 nuns.(6) The nine Coptic monasteries that survive to today have provided leadership for the Coptic church. Of the 117 Patriarchs of the Coptic Church between 412 A.D. and 1988, 93 were monks. Today, all Coptic patriarchs and bishops are chosen from the monasteries.(7)

The spread of monasticism to Europe was influenced, and sometimes initiated, by Egyptian monks. The spread of Christianity to England and Ireland was initiated by Egyptian monks. In fact, Irish Christianity is regarded as "the child of the Egyptian Church."(8)

NOTES

1) Meyer, Robert T. Translator. *St. Athanasius The life of St. Anthony*, (Newman Press, New York, NY 1950) p. 3.
2) Ibid., p. 5.
3) Latourette, Kenneth Scott. *A History of Christianity Vol.I*, (Harper & Row, Publishers, New York, NY 1975) p. 226.
4) Kamil, Jill. *Coptic Egypt History and Guide*, (The American University in Cairo Press, Cairo Egypt 1987) pp. 39-40.
5) Latourette, *A History of Christianity Vol.I*, p. 227.
6) Kamil, *Coptic Egypt History and Guide*, pp. 47-48.
7) Watterson, Barbara. *Coptic Egypt*, (Scottish Academic Press, Edinburgh, 1988) p. 76.
8) Meinardus, Otto F.A. *Christian Egypt Ancient and Modern*, (The American University in Cairo, 1977) pp. 23-24.

CHAPTER 13

PRESERVERS OF THE SCRIPTURES

The Bible is unique in several special ways. Unlike most books, it is comprised of many different books by many different writers. It covers more than 3,000 years of history. All of the original manuscripts of the biblical books were either destroyed or lost. It has been revised more than 20 times over the last 1,900 years. It has been translated into hundreds of languages. It is one of the most widely distributed books in the world.

If it is true that all of the writers of the biblical books were Israelites/Jews, then it is true that all of these books were written by black men. It is unlikely that they were white, yet they are popularly perceived as such.

It is also true that the translating of the original manuscripts was done in Africa. The 39 Old Testament books were first translated and compiled from different Hebrew writings in Alexandria, Egypt. This compilation became known as the *Septuagint*, which is interpreted as "seventy." According to tradition, around 250 B.C. 72 Jewish scholars met in Alexandria for 72 days to translate the Pentateuch (the first five books of the Old Testament) into Koine, a vernacular of Greek. However, it took more than 200 years for Alexandrian Jews to translate all of the Hebrew writings.(1) The 27 New Testament books were first compiled by Athanasius, Bishop of Alexandria, in 367 A.D. Therefore, the 66 canonical books of the Bible were first compiled in Africa.

Between 375 and 395 A.D., the New Testament books were translated into the Coptic (which means Egyptian) language by Egyptian monks. This language was developed by transliterating Egyptian sounds into the Greek alphabet and by adding seven Egyptian alphabets for sounds not represented by Greek letters. The Coptic translations of the New Testament were written specifically for the large Egyptian Christian population. The colloquial form of this translation made the New Testament accessible to the Egyptian masses that did not read Koine (Greek).

It is interesting to note the translators chose the word Nute to identify God. Nute is the Coptic form of Netcherw. The Netcherw, from which the word nature is derived, represents the many aspects of the one Supreme God in Egyptian Cosmogony.(2)

Scriptural manuscripts were widely distributed and discussed among early Christians in North Africa. During certain periods of Roman persecution, scriptural documents were confiscated and destroyed. One of the most severe instances was around 300 A.D. during the persecution of Emperor Diocletian. Some presbyters turned over their manuscripts to save their lives. After the persecution ended, and Constantine declared toleration of Christianity, those church leaders who turned over the sacred books were viewed as traitors. This sparked the Donatist controversy, a movement led by Donatus, Bishop of Carthage, to declare the religious authority of the traitors as invalid.(3)

Millions of Greek, Coptic and Arabic papyrus documents were destroyed by excavations of Egypt.(4) Despite the destruction of scriptural and other Christian literature from

140

Africa, many important documents have survived.

The three oldest existing biblical manuscripts are the *Vatican Manuscript*, named so because it is kept at the Vatican; the *Sinaitic Manuscript*, which was originally found in a monastery on Mt Sinai; and the *Alexandrian Manuscript*, which was written in Alexandria.(5) British scholars B.F. Westcott and F.H. Hort developed a system to classify all biblical manuscripts. Four families of classification are produced from this system. They are the *Western Text*, the *Alexandrian Text*, the *Neutral Text* and the *Koine or Byzantine Text*. The *Caesarean Text* was added to this system by later scholars.

The Vatican Manuscript (classified as Codex B), the Sinaitic Manuscript (classified as Codex Aleph) and the Alexandrian Manuscript (classified as Codex A) are all categorized into the Alexandrian Text family. Manuscripts classified in the Alexandrian Text family were widely quoted by such Alexandrian church fathers as Clement, Origen and Cyril. It is reasonable to hypothesize that the popular use of these types of manuscripts among African church leaders indicates that they originated in Alexandria.(6)

Since 1876 there have been more than 40 major works published on Coptic documents that have been found in Egypt. The most significant find was in 1945, when 52 papyrus text were found near Nag Hammadi in the Egyptian desert. They are called the *Nag Hammadi Library*. These Coptic writings date back to the 2nd and maybe the 1st century. They are original Coptic translations of various gnostic gospels and other secret texts. It is likely they were hidden because they were considered heretical. Previously unknown gospels included in the Nag

Hammadi Library are the *Gospel of Thomas*, the *Gospel of Truth* and the *Gospel of the Egyptians*.(7)

NOTES

1) Harris, Stephen L. *Understanding the Bible*, (Mayfield Publishing Company, Palo Alto, CA 1980) pp. 7-8.
2) Latourette, Kenneth Scott. *A History of Christianity Vol.I*, (Harper & Row Publishers, New York, NY 1975) pp. 250-251 and
   Kamil, Jill. *Coptic Egypt History and Guide*, (The American University in Cairo Press, Cairo, Egypt 1987) pp. 46-47.
3) Bainton, Roland H. *Early Christianity*, (Robert E. Krieger Publishing, Florida, 1984) pp. 64-65.
4) Pearson, Birger A. and James E. Goering, Editors. *The Roots of Egyptian Christianity*, (Fortress Press, Philadelphia, PA 1986) p. 44.
5) Lightfoot, Neil R. *How We Got the Bible*, (Baker Book House, Grand Rapids, MI 1963) pp. 30-34.
6) Koester, Helmut. *History and Literature of Early Christianity*, (Walter de Gruyter, New York, NY 1987) pp. 17-18.
7) Pagels, Elaine. *The Gnostic Gospels*, (Random House, New York, NY 1979) p. 14.

CHAPTER 14

AFRICAN MARTYRS

Throughout its first 300 years, Christianity was not an authorized religion of the Roman government. The persecuting of Christians took many different forms. Some emperors expressed little concern about the Christians, while others used deadly force to persecute them. These periods of persecution were usually sparked by lies told about Christian beliefs and practices. They also resulted from the government's attempts to maintain consistency and uniformity of beliefs throughout the empire.

During the 1st century, most of the Apostles were violently put to death. Bartholomew's skin was ripped from his body, James (the son of Zebedee) and Paul were beheaded, and Philip and Peter were crucified. Many more Christians were put to death throughout the Roman Empire. The reports of bravery among African martyrs are quite inspiring. One such account is of 12 Numidians who were executed in Carthage on July 17, 180 A.D. Their leader was a 22-year-old African woman named Perpetua. Her courage was proven when she personally directed the weapon of an inexperienced executioner against her own breast. The story of her bravery spread throughout North Africa.(1)

In 202 A.D. Emperor Septimus Severus, who was an African, issued an edict forbidding Christians and Jews from making new converts. Violators were subject to banishment or forced labor in the imperial mines. Many Christians chose death. Many African martyrs were produced from this period of persecution. Several students of the Catechetical school were put to death, including Plutarch; Serenus, who was burned to death; Heraclides and Hero (a derivative of the name Heru or Horus), both of whom were beheaded; another Serenus, who was tortured to death with an axe; and Herais, a woman burned to death.

Another African woman who gained fame for her courage in defending her faith was Potamiaena. Eusebius described her as having "chastity and virginity, which were beyond reproach." The Roman judge, Aquila, subjected Potamiaena's whole body to painful agony, and also threatened to allow the gladiators to rape her. She was brutally tortured before she and her mother were burned to death. Many Alexandrian Christians claimed they had visions of Potamiaena before they openly affirmed their conversion to Christianity and were put to death.(2)

In 250 A.D. the Emperor Decius initiated another period of persecution. Dionysius, Bishop of Alexandria, reported of many Africans put to death in Alexandria before the official edict was given by Decius. He wrote about an old man named Metras, who was brutally clubbed before pointed reeds were driven into his eyes and face. He was then stoned to death. Also killed was a woman named Quinta, who was dragged through the streets and then stoned to death. In the case of an elder Christian woman named Apollonia, who refused to recite "heathen incantations," and her persecutors knocked out all of her teeth. While still being tortured, she asked for breathing space. When they released her, she jumped to her death into a raging fire that had been prepared for her.

When the official edict came, many other Africans were put to death. Those who suffered in this wave of persecutions to name a few included a Libyan named Macar, who was burned to death; and four women, Ammonarion, Mercuria, Dionysia, and another Ammonarion, all of whom died by the sword.(3) Some Christians hid themselves in the desert and mountains and many died from starvation or wild beasts.

The final and most severe period of persecution came in 304 A.D. and was instigated by Galarius and issued by Maximian, who were joint Emperors with Diocletian. Eusibius reports of Africans enduring outrageous agonies in Thebaid. These Christians were "torn to bits from head to foot with potsherds like claws."(4) Women were tortured by being hoisted in the air naked with a rope tied to only one foot. For years, many men, women and children were put to death. In 311 A.D. the persecutions were ended by Galarius, who was dying of a painful disease.

These black men and women suffered brutal persecution without resorting to violence to save themselves. They perfected the concept of non-violent resistance more than 1,600 years before Dr. Martin Luther King popularized the concept in the 20th century.

NOTES

1) degraft-Johnson, J.C. *African Glory*, (Black Classic Press, Baltimore, MD 1954) pp. 32,40-41.
2) Williamson, G.A., Translator. *Eusebius The History of the Church From Christ to Constantine*, (Augsburg Publishing House, Minneapolis, MN 1965) pp. 244-246.
3) Ibid., pp. 275-278.
4) Ayerst, David and A.S.T. Fisher, *Records of Christianity*, (Basil Blackwell, Oxford) p. 137.

CHAPTER 15

COPTIC AND CATHOLIC SPLIT

During its first 500 years, the leaders of the Christian church tried to establish one universal church with a consistent doctrine. The word "catholic" means universal, and was used to describe this concept of a unified Christian church. This consistency was never reached. In fact, the conflicts grew.

There were many different theological, social and political issues that contributed to the splitting of the church. Some of the factors included the attempts of Bishops of Rome and Alexandria to gain supremacy over other sees; factionalism produced from diverse theological perspectives; and political manipulation of the church by imperial authorities.

Though there were many factors that led to the split, the conflicts produced by the Arian controversy were the major cause. It started around 324 A.D. in Alexandria when an Egyptian presbyter named Arius conflicted with Alexander, Bishop of Alexandria, regarding the teachings of Origen on the nature of Christ. Alexander's successor, Athanasius, became the champion in confronting Arius' views.

Origen taught of the "eternal, timeless generation" of the Son of God, but he made the Son (Jesus) subordinate to the Father (God). Arius supported the idea of a subordinate relationship and rejected the concept of an eternal generation. He stated that a "generation" cannot be "timeless." Arius asserted that there was a point in time when the generation of Christ started, giving him a point of beginning. He taught that Jesus was the "first born" of all creation, God's agent in the creation of all else and subject to change because he was a created being. This

149

description of the Son is identical to the description of Amen in Egyptian mythology, and may be one reason why it was rejected by many as heretical.

Athanasius argued that if the Son is not eternally the Son, then neither is the Father's role eternal. If the Son is subject to change, there is no sure ground for the doctrine of eternal salvation. In 325 A.D. the Council of Nicea declared Arianism as heretical and concluded that "the Son is one being, or essence, or substance with the Father, and those that say that he was made out of nothing, or that his being is different from that of the Father are anathema."(1)

The issue did not end. It smoldered and eventually grew into a raging controversy that completed the splitting of the church. The decision reached at the Council of Nicea was reversed at an Arian-controlled council meeting held in Tyre in 335 A.D. In 356 A.D. opponents of Arianism were forced into exile by the Emperor Constantius, who was an Arian. This period of exile ended in 361 A.D. and another short period of exile began in 364 A.D.

In 381 A.D. Emperor Theodosius I, a strict Christian orthodox against Arianism, held a council meeting at Constantinople. This council reaffirmed the Nicene Creed and officially added the Holy Spirit to the Father and Son to complete the trinity of three uncreated aspects of the one God. They also recognized the See of Alexandria as subordinate to the See of Constantinople, which was made a major center for Christianity by Constantine.(2) This council meeting displeased many African church leaders and helped to further strengthen a nationalistic fervor that always existed among many of the African church leaders.

The next stage of the controversy involved Nestorius, Bishop of Constantinople, and Cyril, Bishop of Alexandria. In 430 A.D. Cyril held a local council in Alexandria to challenge Nestorius' teachings that "the Virgin" Mary was the *Christotokos* (Christ-bearing or Mother of Christ), conflicting with a more popular belief in Mary as the *Theotokos* (God-bearing or Mother of God).

A general council of all church bishops was called in 431 A.D. by Emperor Theodosius II and held in Ephesus. Cyril had the support of the Bishops of African sees and Ephesus. Supporters of Nestorius arrived several days late. The supporters of Cyril seized this opportunity to condemn and depose Nestorius. When supporters of Nestorius arrived, they protested the council's decision. The matter was presented to the Emperor, who temporarily deposed Cyril and Nestorius. It was decided in 433 A.D. that Jesus was "true God and true man, consisting of a reasonable soul and a body."(3) Nestorius remained exiled in Egypt until his death in 444.

In 449 A.D. a monk named Eutyches from Constantinople challenged the decision reached in 433. He denounced the decision as Nestorianism. In 449 Theodosius II called the bishops to a council meeting in Ephesus. Eutyches taught that before the union (incarnation), there were two natures, divine and human. These natures became one, after the union. Eutyches was opposed by Flavian, Bishop of Constantinople, and supported by Dioscurus, Bishop of Alexandria. The council upheld the opinion of Eutyches. Dioscurus, who presided over the council, excommunicated the Bishops of Rome, Antioch and Constantinople. The losers in this conflict called the meeting the "Robber Council." However, this victory was short lived.

151

In 451 A.D. Marcian, the successor to Theodosius II, called the bishops to another council meeting in Chalcedon. This meeting was the last major council of the church before the split. This council concluded that the son was perfect in "Godhead" and perfect in "manhood," truly God and truly man. This acknowledgement of two natures is called the Diphysite view. The council further concluded that the Son and Father were of the same substance (*homoousion*); that the son was without sin and the only-begotten of the Father; and that the Virgin was the Mother of God (*Theotokos*).

Eutyches was denounced as a heretic and Dioscurus was deposed and excommunicated. This council also established a church hierchy, recognizing Rome as the superior see and Constantinople as the second in authority.

The decisions reached at Chalcedon produced a fatal split between the eastern sees of Alexandria, Antioch and Jerusalem, from the western sees of Rome and Constantinople. Throughout the next 200 years, the Egyptian church developed its own independent structure separate from the politically enforced "Catholic" church. The term "Coptic" is popularly used to distinguish this branch of Christianity. "Coptic" or "Copt" is derived from the Greek *Aiguptious*, a word used to identify the Egyptians, separate from the Greeks and other nationalities living in Egypt.

The Coptic Church maintained a Monophysite view, recognizing the Father and Son as one nature. The Monophysite doctrine had some supporters from time to time in other parts of the Christian world, but it was recognized as a belief consistent with Egyptian nationalism. Those few Egyptians who were Diphysites were regarded as *Melkites* or the king's Christians. They composed the membership of the Orthodox Church in Egypt. The majority of Egyptian Christians belonged to the Coptic Church.

Attempts to suppress the Coptic Church continued from 451 A.D. until the rise of Islam in 642. Islam presented a serious challenge to Coptic Christianity. Many Copts accepted Islam, while others were forced south into Ethiopia. Athanasius appointed Frumentarius, a Syrian, as the first bishop of the church in Ethiopia in the 4th century. This church provided a place of refuge for Coptic Christians.

The Coptic and Orthodox Christians who remained in Egypt were forced to pay large taxes to the Islamic rulers and they had to wear distinctive clothing to make them easy to recognize. Under Islamic rule, the Christians were not allowed to build new churches, ring the church bell, display the cross in public or ride a horse. There was no pressure to conform to a specific form of Christianity because they were all given the same rights.(4) In 705 A.D. the Copts were forced to use the Arabic language instead of the Coptic language.

Towards the end of the 10th century, a new dynasty of Moslem rulers, the Fatimids, gained power in Egypt from the Addasid, Caliph of Baghdad. In the beginning, they eased restrictions against the Christians, some of whom reached high positions in government. However, around 1200 A.D., the Caliph Hakim began a period of Christian persecution. Following generations brought varying degrees of persecution.(5) In the 12th century, most Egyptian and Ethiopian Christians belonged to the Coptic Church.

Islam has remained as the dominant religion in Egypt, as about 90 percent of the Egyptians are Moslems. At the end of the 19th century, there were approximately 500,000 Coptic Christians. Today there are more than 4.7 million Coptic Christians, most living in Ethiopia. Many of their original customs have survived, such as the ceremonial use of the Coptic language; their calendar, based of the flow of the Nile River; circumcision; and burial customs.(6)

The growth of Coptic Christianity beyond Africa is not clear. The Rastafarians of Jamaica were influenced by the Ethiopian Coptic Faith, a church formed in Jamaica by Joseph N. Hibbert. There are several Coptic churches in America. In the 1950s Prophet Melchizedek (Louis Cicero Patterson) founded the Universal Prayer House and Training School, on the south side of Chicago, IL. After his death, his work was continued by Prophet Peter (Eddie Banks), who founded the True Temple of Solomon, which continues to be an active Coptic church in Chicago, and his ministry ultimately produced 10 Coptic churches in America. The migration of Coptic Christians throughout the world and increased awareness of Kemitic (Egyptian) beliefs, may cause an increased interest in Coptic Christianity.

The supremacy of the Roman Catholic Church was not easily attained. Its contributions to early Christianity were few. The popular perception is that it began with the Apostle Peter as its first pope, and remained as the superior see from the first century. However, the truth is its early Christian community was very small. The spread of Christianity began with the Jewish communities of the empire. The earliest record of a Jewish community in Rome dates back to 139 B.C.(7) At the same time, there were more than a million Jews living in Egypt. In the 1st century there were only 40,000 to 50,000 Jews living in Rome. There were also times when the Emperor expelled Jews from Rome in 19 A.D. and in 49 A.D. These expulsions decreased the Jewish population there.(8)

Regarding claims that the Apostle Peter founded the See of Rome, there is no evidence that this ever happened. In fact, this belief in Peter as the first Roman Pope began in the 3rd century and was used as justification for claiming religious supremacy over the entire Christian world. It is likely that he was martyred in Rome, where he was buried near Vatican Hill around 64 A.D. According to Raymond E. Brown, co-author of *Antioch & Rome New Testament Cradles of Catholic Christianity*, "We have no knowledge at all of when he [Peter] came to Rome and what he did there before he was martyred. Certainly he was not the original missionary who brought Christianity to Rome (and therefore not the founder of the church of Rome in that sense). There is no serious proof that he was the bishop (or local ecclesiastical officer) of the Roman church, a claim not made until the third century."(9)

The earliest record of Christians in Rome comes from Tacitus, who states that the Christians were blamed for a fire that burned most of Rome in 64 A.D. Tacitus reports that Emperor Nero had these Christians attacked by dogs and used them as human torches.(10) The presence of a distinct community of Christians in Rome in 64 A.D. and references to the Roman Church made by Paul indicate that the church began around 50 A.D.

The term "catholic," which means universal, was used collectively to describe all of the sees. It is now used to describe all of the churches founded under the authority of the Roman church, headed by its bishop or pope. It was Pope Leo I (440

155

to 461 A.D.) who popularized the belief that the Roman pope solely held the authority of Christ. He argued that this authority was first given to Peter and then passed on through the bishops of the Roman church. Later popes also used a document, then believed to be authentic, called the *Donations of Constantine*. The Roman church claimed that Emperor Constantine donated his palace in Rome, the city of Rome and all of Italy to the church to express his gratitude to Sylvester I, the Bishop of Rome, who converted, baptized and healed him of leprosy. This document was later identified as a forgery.(11)

The claims of superiority made by the Roman church resulted in another split that produced the Greek Orthodox or Eastern Orthodox Church in the 13th century. Since the Council of Chalcedon, this eastern (Constantinople) branch of the church grew distant from the western (Roman) branch. Many factors contributed to this split; factors that don't directly relate to the purpose of this book.

The growth of the Roman Catholic Church throughout the world resulted from its connections to various imperial or political powers. Most recently, it has suffered financial difficulties; controversies about sexual abuse; theological controversies (e.g. the ordination of women, celibacy of the priest and marriage of priest); a decline in parishioners; and a serious decline in recruitment of new priests.

NOTES

1) Bainton, Roland H. *Early Christianity*, (Robert E. Krieger Publishing, Florida, 1984) p. 68.
2) Latourette, Kenneth Scott. *A History of Christianity Vol. I*, (Harper & Row, Publishers, New York, NY 1975) p. 164 and Watterson, Barbara. *Coptic Egypt*, (Scottish Academic Press, Edinburgh, 1988) p. 42.
3) Latourette, *A History of Christianity Vol.I*, p. 168.
4) Davis, Leo Donald. *The First Seven Ecumenical Councils (325-787)*, (Michael Glazier, Inc., Wilmington, DE 1987) p. 269.
5) Latourette, *A History of Christianity Vol.I*, pp. 586-587.
6) Latourette, Kenneth Scott. *The History of the Expansion of Christianity*, (Harper & Brothers, New York, NY 1944)
7) Brown, Raymond E. and John P. Meier. *Antioch & Rome New Testament Cradles of Catholic Christianity*, (Paulist Press, New York, NY 1982) p. 93.
8) Ibid., pp. 94-95.
9) Ibid., p. 98.
10) Watterson, *Coptic Egypt*, p. 19.
11) Granfield, Patrick. *The Papacy in Transition*, (Gill and MacMillan, Dublin 1981) p. 5 (footnote 8).

CHAPTER 16

HOW CHRISTIANITY WAS COLORED WHITE

Friedrich Nietzsche, a well known philosopher, wrote the following about history:

> History is necessary to the man of conservative and reverent nature, who looks back to the origins of his existence with love and trust; through it he gives thanks for life. He is careful to preserve what survives from ancient days, and will reproduce the conditions of his own upbringing for those who come after him; thus he does life a service. The possessions of his ancestors' furniture changes its meaning in his soul; for his soul is rather possessed by it....The history of his town becomes the history of himself; he looks on the walls, the turreted gates, the town council, the fair, as an illustrated diary of his youth, and sees himself in it all.(1)

It was this approach to history that guided the early European church in its recreation of Christian/biblical history. The distorting of history and creating of white biblical characters was done to allow the European the opportunity to see himself in his Christian heritage, as himself. The exclusion of true black images from the Europeans' interpretation of biblical events was a by-product of their attempts to see themselves in a history that seldom included their race. The racism that infects the minds of the present generations did not exist in early Christianity. This present form of racism is represented by the belief that people of the lightest hues are superior to people of the darkest hues. This form of racism is represented by the distorting of history to create a false past to justify a false present, which will inevitably lead to more confusion and hatred in the future.

To recreate historical figures in ways that alter the facts of the past cannot be called history. It falls into the category of myth. Biblical history has been altered in many different ways for many different reasons. To embellish and hyperbolize a historical event in order to make clear the lessons to be learned from past events is often harmless and can be a good thing. To distort historical events to create an advantage for one group of people, while creating disadvantage for another group, is evil, careless, reckless and mean-spirited.

Sometime within the last 2,000 years the motives of European historians changed from trying to include themselves in the biblical story to trying to completely exclude black (or dark hued) people from the biblical story. This process of exclusion directly contributed to the formation of the past form of racism that identified black people as inhuman. This process of exclusion directly contributed to the brutal slave trade and colonialism that has almost destroyed black people. This process of exclusion directly contributes to the present form of racism that gives whites a sense of superiority and blacks a sense of inferiority.

The use of white images as biblical/Christian characters probably started in the 4th century when Christianity became the official religion of the Roman Empire. The imperial Roman commitment to Christianity was based on the need for the empire to have a uniform religious belief system. Christianity was not chosen as the state religion because of Constantine's belief in Jesus. He continued to worship other gods long after his "conversion" to Christianity. By combining some idolatrous beliefs with Christian beliefs, the Roman government attempted to make Christianity acceptable to the masses of people under Roman rule.

For this reason Isis and Horus were equated with Mary and Jesus; Serapis, Osiris and Horus were equated with Jesus; the festivals of Ishtar and Mithra were given Christian imagery, and celebrated as Easter and Christmas; and the ankh (the Kemitic symbol for life) was equated with the cross. The image of Serapis and some white images of Jesus are very similar. Serapis was the creation of Ptolemy I, made around 300 B.C. through merging Osiris with Apis, a Memphite god. Worship of Serapis was popular among some people of Alexandria, but was widely rejected by Jews and most Egyptians. Walter Williams, author of *The Historical Origin of Christianity*, argued that the Serapis image was used to depict Jesus in the 4th century.(2) It is likely that the Serapis image was widely used to represent Jesus among Roman (Gentile) Christians, but not among Coptic Christians.

Most of the portraits, paintings, carvings and sculptures of biblical figures were produced more than 400 years after biblical times by European artists. There is a suspicious lack of archaeological evidence depicting Jews and Palestinians who lived during the early Christian era. Most of the few existing images depict them as black or dark-skinned people.

From the 14th to 16th centuries, a period of Christian art produced many white images of biblical characters. Some of the artists involved in this period were Fra Angelico (1387-1455), Giotto (1267-1337), Donatello (1386-1466), and Filippo Lippi (1406-1469). The most notable artists of this period were

Raphael (1483-1520) and Michelangelo (1475-1564).

In 1508 Raphael and Michelangelo were commissioned by Pope Julius II to paint biblical images. Works produced by Raphael include *Christ Bearing the Cross*, *Madonna*, *Holy Family*, and *The Marriage of Joseph and the Virgin*. He also such painted frescoes in the Vatican as *The Fall of Adam* and *Solomon's Judgement*.

The paintings by Michelangelo on the ceilings of the Sistine Chapel are regarded as a masterpiece of decorative design. This series includes the *History of Moses*, the *Life of Christ*, the *Creation*, the *History of Noah*, the *Prophets* and the *Last Judgement*.

These images were later printed in large illustrated King James Versions of the Bible and passed on by families, from one generation to the next. For many people, these were the earliest biblical images to which they were introduced. These images are also recreated in paintings, mosaics and stained glass in thousands of churches throughout the world. Many Christians believe that biblical people spoke in an old English dialect, using "thee," "art," "lo" and "thou." This was not the way that the people of Bible spoke. The ancient Israelites spoke Hebrew or Aramaic.

Most impressive and popular are the motion pictures of biblical events. Since the late 1950s, new films are made each year, depicting the biblical figures as white. Billions of people have been exposed to these images that, while blatantly glorifying the biblical characters, subtlely glorify the race of the white actors playing the biblical characters.

A major contributing factor to the confusion regarding the race of the ancient and 1st century Israelites is the fact that modern Jews of today are white. It is logical to conclude that if the majority of those people who are called Jews are white, then their ancestors were white. If these white Jews are the descendants of the ancient Israelites, then the ancient Israelites were white. However, the ancient Israelites were not white, they were black. As black people, their genetic dominance should produce black or dark hued descendants. In order for the ancient Jews to have become a white people, they would have had to undergo a genetic mutation. This was not the case.

Though the majority of modern Jews are actual Jews, they are not Semitic descendants of the ancient Israelites. The two main types of modern Jews are Ashkenazi and Sephardim. More than 90 percent of those people who identify themselves as Jews are Ashkenazi Jews. Less than 6% are Sephardim Jews. The word "Sephardim" comes from the Hebrew word "Sepharad," which means Spain, and is used to identify the Jews who descended from ancestors that lived in Spain until the 15th century. In the 1960s, there were about 500,000 Sephardim Jews.

The actual meaning of Ashkenazi is unclear. The Hebrew word Ashkenaz was used to refer to Germany. The Bible identifies Ashkenaz as the name for a grandson of Japheth. Ashkenazi is used in general to identify those Jews who descended from ancestors who lived in Eastern Europe. There were about 11 million Ashkenazi Jews during the 1960s.(3)

It is now widely believed that Ashkenazi Jewry originated with a Turkish people called the Khazars. The Khazar Empire accepted Judaism as the state religion, the same as Rome chose

Christianity. In 740 A.D. the Khazars chose Judaism for the sake of neutrality. The choice of Judaism allowed them to maintain their sovereignty without choosing Christianity or Islam as their official religion. Either religion would have made them subject to an established religious hierchy. Judaism had no religious or political hierchy, but was the foundation from which the other two religions came.(4)

For more than 600 years after their conversion, the Khazars observed Judaism as their official religion. The decline of the Khazar Empire began in 965 A.D. when they were defeated by the Russians. They were allowed to remain independent, and continued to practice their Jewish beliefs into the 13th century. The disappearance of the Khazars from their original homeland (north of the Black Sea, Caucausoid Mountains and Caspian Sea) happened at the same time that Jewish immigrants settled in Germany and Poland.

The vast majority of those people who identify themselves as Jews descended from these Eastern European, or Ashkenazi, Jews. They are Jews but, they are not Hebrews or Israelites by descent. When considering the ancient Israelites (the original 12 tribes), it must be remembered that most of them lost their Israelite heritage before the 1st century. After the 1st century, many Jews became Christians or were later persecuted by the Romans. When Christianity became the official religion of the Roman Empire, the Christians began to persecute Jews and other "pagan" people. During this time, Jews migrated to many different parts of the world. Some even migrated to Khazaria and probably participated in the converting of Khazaria, making it the first independent Jewish kingdom since 586 B.C.

Jose V. Malcioln, author of *How the Hebrews Became Jews*, provides the following categories for modern Jewry:

Ashkenazim - Descendants and admixtures of Hebrews and even Gentiles. Others are proselytes converted several centuries ago.

Sephardim - Hebrews of North Africa, Syria, Spain, Portugal, Egypt, Turkey, Arabia, the West Indies and Latin America.

Falashim - Hebrews of North, East and West Africa, particularly Ethiopia.(5)

The Falashim Jews are the most obvious descendants of the Israelites. These black people claim direct descent from the ancient Israelites and possess ancient Hebrew documents, a claim that cannot be made by Ashkenazi Jews. For more than 2,000 years, there have been rumors that the Ark of the Covenant is in Ethiopia. The Ark was made of precious metals and stones by the Israelites and used to store the tablets of laws made by Moses. It is believed that the Ark is kept in a temple in the ancient city of Axum and is guarded by a secretive order of monks. Graham Hancock, author of *The Sign and the Seal: The Quest for the Lost Ark of the Covenant*, claimed that he located the Ark in Axum. He also revealed the efforts of "a shadowy group of Freemasons" who descended from the Templars (a secret society that began in the 12th century as an order of Christian knights) in their plot to obtain the Ark.(6)

The opinion that Christianity is the "white man's religion," and that the Bible was written by "the white man," became a popular statement of black cultural nationalists during the 1960s. Despite efforts, sincere or insincere, to "whitewash" Christianity, it is still a religion that began with black people, and is to be shared by all people who want to be like Christ.

NOTES

1) Nietzsche, Friedrich. *The Use and Abuse of History*, (The Liberal Arts Press, New York, NY 1949) p. 25.
2) Williams, Walter. *The Historical Origin of Christianity*, (Maathian Press, Inc. Chicago, IL 1992) p. iii   and Kamil, Jill. *Coptic Egypt History and Guide*, (The American University in Cairo Press, Cairo Egypt 1987) p. 20.
3) Koestler, Arthur. *The Thirteenth Tribe*, (Hutchinson & Co. Publishers, London 1976) p. 181.
4) Ibid., pp. 59-60.
5) Malcioln, Jose V. *How the Hebrews Became Jews*, (U.B. Productions, New York, NY 1978) p. 13.
6) *Biblical Archaeology Review*, "Is the Ark of the Covenant in Ethiopia?" by Ephraim Isaac, July/August 1993, pp. 60-63.

CHAPTER 17

CHRISTIANS RECLAIMING AFRICENTRISM

According to Luke 4:18, Jesus said, "The Spirit of the Lord is upon me, because he hath anointed me to preach the Gospel to the poor; he hath sent me to heal the brokenhearted, to preach deliverance to the captive, and recovering of sight to the blind, to set at liberty them that are bruised."

Christianity is supposed to be a religion based on the life, example, and Gospel of the biblical Jesus Christ. This Jesus spoke of preaching the Gospel to the poor, but the Europeans have used the Gospel to create poverty and hunger throughout the world.(1) They used their religious authority to justify slavery and colonialism upon which their economic systems are built. A popular saying among many Africans is "When the white man first came, he had his Bible, and we had our land. Now, we have his Bible, and he has our land." In the name of "Jesus," we (as African people) have been robbed of our traditional ways, and made to think that African traditions and culture are inferior, uncivilized or evil. We have been made to think that the Europeans' interpretations of Christianity are superior, civilized and the only way to salvation.(2)

Jesus spoke of bringing deliverance to the captive and setting at liberty the bruised. Yet the Roman Catholic Church used its wealth and power to support the enslavement of African people. They used their powers to colonize the world under European rulership. They created more captives and bruised rather than creating more liberty and justice. Like a bad little boy that throws a rock and then hides his hands, the Eurocentered Christian world is directly responsible for the poverty, warfare,

169

sickness and death affecting African and aboriginal people, and in taking the lands that they conquered in the name of manifest destiny. Now they try to make themselves look like the innocent humanitarians and peacemakers of the world. The Christianized European nations of the world claim that they want to create a "New World Order" of peace and prosperity, while they simultaneously and secretly plan a new era of colonialism and legal slavery.(3)

The world is in serious trouble. There is fear that nuclear war could occur any day. The industries of the world have polluted the land, water and air with toxic chemicals and plastics. The nations of the world are constantly in conflict with each other. Religion has become "the opiate of the people," making us passive and insensitive to the realities around us. In some strangely evil way, the very teachings that can bring us more life and liberty have been used to do the opposite. This must be a false presentation of Christianity, and false religions are the real opiates of the masses. True Christianity is a religion of liberation. The fact that biblical history is African centered by nature is obvious. If the Bible represents the truth of God's relationship with man, then God must have a reason for establishing Christianity with black people. We insult the wisdom of God when we tell "a little white lie" about the ethnicity of the people of the Bible.

I have personally experienced the reality and power of the Word of God (which is much more than a book), having been brought up in a Christian family, and being a servant of God through the example and salvation offered through Jesus Christ. My commitment, understanding and submission to the will of God has been multiplied through my learning the

170

culture of my (African) people. The culture, history and spirituality of Africa complements my Christianity. I am a much better Christian because of my African ways.

The world has been led to believe that anything African is inferior and backwards. The truth is, the very place that the world has been taught to reject is the cradle of humanity and civilization. If Africa is so bad, why did God produce humanity there? If African beliefs are so evil, why are many of the beliefs re-introduced to us through the Bible and Christian theology?

For hundreds of years, black people have believed Jesus and all of the biblical figures were white. Many of our black families have portraits of a "white Jesus" in our homes and churches. Can Christians of all races now accept the reality of a black Jesus, the same as non-Europeans have accepted the white image? Will some Christians reject Jesus because he is black? Has racism become more important to Christians than their submission to God? Many Christians expect the return of Jesus in his physical form. If this happens, and Jesus returns in his original black form, will Christians reject their place in God's kingdom because the one sent to lead them is black?

Christians must accept the fact that historical Christianity is African-centered. Jesus spoke of "recovering of sight to the blind." European-centered Christianity has been used to blind and confuse the masses. When a student learns only half of what the teacher presents, that student is only half informed. If that student becomes an architect, he will have just enough information to design a building that will collapse and kill anyone in the building. Christians must examine the African aspects of Christianity in order to design a life based on the whole truth.

171

NOTES

1) Hayter, Teresa. *The Creation of World Poverty*, (Pluto Press, London 1990) pp. 40-46   and
   Cone, James H. *The Black Theology & Black Power*, (The Seabury Press, New York, NY 1969) p. 71.
2) Ani, Marimba. *Yurugu An African-Centered Critique of European Cultural Thought and Behavior*, (African World Press, Trenton, NJ 1994) p. 186.
3) Mullins, Eustace. *The World Order*, (Ezra Pound Institute of Civilization, Staunton, VA 1985) pp. 201-202, 216-217.

BIBLIOGRAPHY

Ani, Marimba. *Yurugu An African-Centered Critigue of European Cultural Thought and Behavior*, (African World Press, Trenton, NJ 1994).

Saint Augustine, *The City of God*, (The Modern Library of Random House, New York, NY 1950).

Ayerst, Davis and A.S.T. Fisher. *Records of Christianity*, (Basil Blackwell, Oxford).

Bainton, Roland H. *Early Christianity*, (Robert E. Krieger Publishing, Florida, 1984).

Benz, Ernst. *The Eastern Orthodox Church*, (Anchor Books of Doubleday & Company, Inc., Garden City, NY 1963).

Bernal, Martin. *Black Athena Vol.2*, (Rutgers University Press, New Brunswick, NJ 1991).

Biblical Archaeology Review, "Is the Ark of the Covenant in Ethiopia?" by Ephraim Isaac, July/August 1993, pp. 60-63.

Boyd, Paul C. *The African Origin of Christianity Vol.I*, (Karia Press, London 1991).

Brown, Raymond E. and John P. Meier. *Antioch and Rome New Testament Cradles of Catholic Christianity*, (Paulist Press, New York, NY 1982).

Browder, Tony. *Nile Valley Contributions to Civilization*, (The Institute for Karmic Guidance, Washington D.C. 1992).

Budge, E.A. Wallis. *The Book of the Dead*, (University Books, Inc., Secaucus, NJ 1960).

Clarke, G.W., Translator. *The Letters of St. Cyprian of Carthage*, (Newmann Press, New York, NY 1950).

Comay, Joan and Ronald Brownrigg. *Who's Who in the Bible*, (Bonanza Books. New York, NY 1980).

175

Cone, James H. *Black Theology & Black Power*, (The Seabury Press, New York, NY 1969).

Conzelmann, Han. *History of Primitive Christianity*, (Abingdon Press, New York, NY 1973).

Copher, Charles B. *Black Biblical Studies*, (Black Light Fellowship, Chicago, IL 1990).

Davis, Leo Donald. *The First Seven Ecumenical Councils (325-787)*, (Michael Glazier, Inc., Wilmington, DE 1987).

Diop, Cheikh Anta. *The African Origin of Civilization*, (Lawrence Hill & Company, Westport 1974).

Diop Chiekh Anta, *Civilization or Barbarism*, (Lawrence Hill Books, Brooklyn, NY 1991).

Diop, Chiekh Anta. *The Cultural Unity of Black Africa*, (Third World Press, Chicago, IL 1978)

Dunston, Bishop Alfred G. Jr. *The Black Man in the Old Testament and its World*, (Africa World Press, Inc., Trenton, NJ 1992).

deGraft-Johnson, J.A. *African Glory*, (Black Classic Press, Baltimore, MD 1954).

Durant, Will. *The Story of Civilization, Part One: Our Oriental Heritage*, (Simon and Schuster, New York, NY 1954).

Felder, Cain Hope, Editor. *Stony the Road We Trod*, (Fortress Press, Minneapolis, MN 1991).

Gottwald, Norman K. *All the Kingdoms of the Earth*, (Harper and Row Publishers, New York, NY 1964).

Granfield, Patrick. *The Papacy in Transition*, (Gill and MacMillan, Dublin 1981).

Grant, Robert, M. *Augustus to Constantine*, (Harper &. Row, Publishers, New York NY 1970).

Grant, Robert M. *Second-Century Christianity*, (The Trustees of the Society for Promoting Christian Knowledge, London 1957).

Griggs, C. Wilfred. *Early Egyptian Christianity From its Orgins to 451 C.E.*, (E.J. Brill, New York, NY 1990).

Groves, C.P. *The Planting of Christianity in Africa*, (Lutterworth Press, London 1948).

Harney, Martin P. *The Catholic Church Through the Ages*, (Daughters of St. Paul, Boston, MA 1974).

Harris, Joseph E., Editor. *Africa and Africans as Seen by Classical Writers*, (Howard University Press, Washington D.C. 1977).

Harris, Stephen L. *Understanding the Bible*, (Mayfield Publishing Company, Palo Alto, CA 1980).

Hayter, Teresa. *The Creation of World Poverty*, (Pluto Press, London 1990).

Kamil, Jill. *Coptic Egypt History and Guide*, (The American University in Cairo Press, Cairo, Egypt 1987).

Koester, Helmut, *History and Literature of Early Christianity Vol.2*, (Walter De Gruyter, New York, NY 1987).

Koestler, Arthur. *The Thirteenth Tribe*, (Hutchinson & Co. Publishers, London 1976).

Insight Magazine, "Tracking Mother of 5000 Tongues" by Harvey Hagman, February 5, 1990, pp. 54-55.

Johnson, John L. *The Black Biblical Heritage*, (Winston-Derek Publishers, Inc., Nashville, TN 1993).

LaHaye, Tim and John Morris. *The Ark on Ararat*, (Thomas Nelson Inc., New York, NY 1976).

Latourette, Kenneth Scott. *A History of Christianity I and II*, (Harper and Row Publishers, New York, NY 1975).

Latourette, Kenneth Scott. *The History of the Expansion of Christianity*, (Harper & Brothers, New York, NY 1944).

Lightfoot, Niel R. *How We Got the Bible*, (Baker Book House, Grand Rapids, MI 1963).

Malcioin, Jose V. *How the Hebrews Became Jews*, (U.B. Productions, New York, NY 1978).

Massey, Gerald. *Book of Beginnings Vol.2*, (Williams and Norgate, London 1881).

Massey, Gerald. *The Historical Jesus and the Mythical Christ*, (A&B Books Publishing, Brooklyn, NY 1992).

Mbiti, John S. *Introduction to African Religion*, (Heinemann Educational Books, London, 1975).

McCray, Rev. Walter Arthur. *The Black Presence in the Bible*, I and II, (Black Light Fellowship, Chicago, IL 1990).

Meinardus, Otto F.A. *Chistian Egypt Ancient and Modern*, (The American University in Cairo Press, Cairo 1977).

Meyer, Robert T., Tranalator. *St. Athanasius The Life of St. Anthony*, (Newman Press, New York NY 1950).

Mosley, William. *What Color Was Jesus?*, (African American Images, Chicago, IL 1987).

Mullins, Eustace. *The World Order*, (Ezra Pound Institute of Civilization, Staunton, VA 1985).

Murphy, Jefferson E. *The History of African Civilization*, (Dell Publishing Co. Inc. New York, NY 1972).

Newsweek, "The Search for Adam and Eve" by John Tierney, January 11, 1988, pp. 46-52.

Nietzsche, Friedrich. *The Use and Abuse of History*, (The Liberal Arts Press, New York, NY 1949).

The Original African Heritage Study Bible, King James Version (The James C. Winston Publishing Company, Nashville TN 1993).

Oulton, John Ernest Leonard and Henry Chadwick, Translators. *Alexandrian Christianity*, (The Westminster Press, Philadelphia, PA).

Pagels, Elaine. *The Gnostic Gospels*, (Random House, New York, NY 1979).

Pamphilus, Eusebius. *Ecclesiastical History*, (Baker Book House, Grand Rapids, MI 1991).

Pearson, Birger A. and James E. Goehring, Editors. *The Roots of Egyptian Christianity*, (Fortress Press, Philadelphia, PA 1986).

Pentecost, J. Dwight. *The Word and Works of Jesus Christ*, (Academie Books of Zondervan Publishing House, Grand Rapids, MI 1981).

Prabhupada, A.C. Bhaktivedanta Swami. *Srimad Bhagavatam sixth Canto Part-One*, (The Bhaktivedanta Book Trust, Los Angeles, CA 1979).

Pritchard, James B. *The Ancient Near East in Pictures*, (Princeton University Press, Princeton, NJ 1954).

Radin, Max. *The Jews Among the Greeks and Romans*, (Jewish Publication Society of America, Philidelphia, PA 1915).

Rogers, J.A. *Sex and Race Vol.1*, (Helga M. Rogers, St. Petersburg, FL 1967).

Saakana, Amon Saba, Editor. *The Afrikan Origin of the Major World Religions*, (Karnak House 1988).

Smith, Morton. *Palestinian Parties and Politics That Shaped the Old Testament*, (SCM Press LTd., London 1987).

U.S. News and World Report, "Who We Were" by William
   Allman, September 16, 1991, pp. 53-60.

Van Sertima, Ivan and Runoko Rashidi, Editors. *African
   Presence in Early Asia*, (Transaction Books, New
   Brunswick, GA 1988).

Watterson, Barbara, *Coptic Egypt*, (Scottish Academic Press,
   Edinburgh, 1988).

Watts, Daud Malik. *The Black Presence in the Land of the
   Bible*, (Afro Vision, Inc., Washington D.C. 1990).

Wells, H.G. *The Outline of History*, (The MacMillan Company,
   New York, NY 1921).

Wheless, Joseph. *Is It God's Word*, (Alfred A. Knopf, New
   York, NY 1926).

Williams, Walter. *The Historical Origin of Christianity*,
   (Maathian Press, Inc., Chicago, IL 1992).

Williamson, G.A., Translator. *Eusebius The History of the
   Church from Christ to Constantine*, (Augsburg Publishing
   House, Minneapolis, MN 1965).

Windsor, Rudolphf R. *The Valley of the Dry Bones*, (Windsor's
   Golden Series, Atlanta, GA 1986).

INDEX

Aaron, 13,48
Abel, 53
Abraham (or Abram),9,19,23-27
Adam and Eve, 105-106
Ahad, 56
Ahasuerus, 57,58
Alexandria, 65
Amen, 14,25-26,47,109
Amenhotep III, 15
Andrew, 90
Antiochus IV Epiphanes, 66-67
Antipater, 68
Antony, 133-135
Apollos, 95-96,100
apostle (or apostolos), 83
Apostle's Creed, 73
Apostles of Jesus, 73-74,86
Aram, 12
Aramaic, 69
Arameans (see Syrians)
Arian controversy, 122,149
Aristobulus II, 67
Arius, 122
Arphaxad, 12
Aryan tongues, 13

Asenath, 41,44
Ashdod, 56
Ashkenazi Jews, 163-165
Ashurbanipal, 15
Asians, 15
Asshur, 12,14
Assyrians, 14-15
Athanasius, 122-123,139
Augustine, 123-125
Babylon, 15, 92,99
Bartholomew, 90
Basilides, 114
Bathsheba, 55
Bel, 13
Benjamin, 9
Bernal, 42-43
Bilhah, 28-29
Black Madonna, 78-79,109
Browder, 47
Brown, 155
Cain, 53,108
Caliph Hakim, 153
Canaan, 11,19-20
Canaanites, 11
canonized, 73

Eutyches, 151
Expected One, 70,75
Ezra, 56,61
Falashim Jews, 165
Fatimids, 153
Finch, 13-14,43,48
Galilee, 65,68,103
Gentiles, 61,84-85,91,92
Gnostics, 114,141
Goshen, 41-42
Goths, 125
Greeks, 60-62
Hagar, 25
Ham, 9,11-12,19-20
Hamitic, 12-15
Hancock, 165
Hansberry, 57
Hasmonian dynasty, 67-68
Heber, 9-10,12
Hebrew, 9
Hecataeus, 60
Hellenistic, 68
Herod, 68
Herodians, 69,70,83
Herodotus, 25

Horus, 101,108-110,161
Hyksos, 41-44
Ireland, 137
Isaac, 27-29,59
Ishmael, 25,27
Isis, 101,107-110,161
Israel, (see Jacob)
Israelites, 11,41-49
Jacob, 9,28-30,41,44
James (son of Alphaeus), 90
James (son of Zebedee), 90
James (the Lord's Brother), 89,95
Japheth, 9,12,163
Jarha, 56
Jephetic, 12
Jesse, 55
Jether, 56
Jews (modern), 163
Jews, 9,58
Jezebel, 56
John Hyrcanus, 67
John, 90-91,86,94
Johoshua ben Pandira, 74
Joseph, 41,48
Josephus, 22,74

ORDER FORM

The Winston-Derek Publishers Group, Inc.

1. *The Original African Heritage Study Bible (KJV)*		$45.00
2. *The Black Biblical Heritage*	John L. Johnson	$24.95
3. *Bible Legacy of the Black Race*	Joyce Andrews	$11.95
4. *100 Amazing Facts on African Presence in the Bible*		$5.95
5. *Blacks Who Died for Jesus*	Mark Hyman	$9.95
6. *Coyle's The New Convert Bible Commentary*	Margaret Coyle	$9.95
7. *Dompim: The Spirituality of African Peoples*	Guerin Montilus	$9.95
8. *Blinds: Distortion of Historical Facts*	Shannon Jolly	$12.95
9. *Winston's Biblical Encyclopedia/Concordance*	J. W. Peebles, Ph.D.	$39.95
10. *Garden of Eden*	Julian Johnson	$3.95
11. *The Preschoolers/Beginners Bible*	V. Gilbert Beers	$15.00
12. *God's Kinship With Dark Colors*	John L. Johnson	$7.95

Quantity	Description	Unit Price

TOTAL DUE (add 5% shipping) $_____

Name_____

Address_____

City _____ State_____ Zip Code_____

Send Payment to:
Winston-Derek Publishers Group, Inc.
P.O. Box 90883, Nashville, Tennessee 37209